THE
127th BATTALION, C.E.F.:
2nd BATTALION, CANADIAN RAILWAY TROOPS

The Naval & Military Press Ltd

Published by
The Naval & Military Press Ltd
5 Riverside, Brambleside, Bellbrook
Industrial Estate, Uckfield, East Sussex,
TN22 1QQ England

Tel: +44 (0) 1825 749494
Fax: +44 (0) 1825 765701

www.naval-military-press.com
www.nmarchive.com

*In reprinting in facsimile from the original, any imperfections are inevitably reproduced
and the quality may fall short of modern type and cartographic standards.*

THE 127th BAT[TALION]

2nd BATTALION, CANA[DIAN]

By the Same Author

The Princess Louise Dragoon Guards.

The Royal Regiment of Artillery (Ottawa)

Rogers' Rangers

Canada's Soldiers, 1604-1954
 (with George F. G. Stanley)

The Queen's Rangers in Upper Canada, 1792 and After.

The Story of the Royal Canadian Dental Corps.

Edited
   The Argyll and Sutherland Highlanders of Canada
   The Queen's Rangers in the Revolutionary War

A Contributor to
   Open House
   The Lincoln and Welland Regiment

Lt.-Col. H. M. Jackson, M.B.E., E.D.

ALION, C.E.F.:
N RAILWAY TROOPS

Colonel F. F. Clarke, D.S.O., M.B.E., V.D.,
Who commanded the 127th Battalion, C.E.F. (2nd Battalion, Canadian Railway Troops), and later The York Rangers (two Battalions).

THEY SERVED IN FRANCE WITH THE 2ND BATTALION, CANADIAN RAILWAY TROOPS

Lt.-Col. J. Murray Muir, V.D., Commanding The York Rangers, 28 Dec. 28 to 31 Dec. 32.

Lt.-Col. John M. Gibson, D.S.O., Commanding The York Rangers, 17 Jul. 23 to 18 Dec. 28.

Major J. C. Boylen, E.D.

TABLE OF CONTENTS

CHAPTER   PAGE

    I In the Somme Area 1
   II Bapaume Operations 15
  III The Fifth Army Area and the Sand Dunes 25
  IV The Messines Offensive 37
   V The Ypres Offensive 49
  VI Advance Camp, Steel Dump 58
 VII Passchendaele 66
VIII Beaumetz and Cugny 81
  IX March, 1918: The German Bid for Victory 92
   X In the Line as Infantry 103
  XI The St. Omer Area 118
 XII The Arras-Albert Area 130
XIII The Roisel-St. Quentin Line 140
XIV St. Quentin-Bohain 151
 XV The Charleroi Area 161

APPENDICES

A. Officers of the 127th Battalion, C.E.F.,
   on embarkation 168
B. The Roll of Honour 169
C. Non-Fatal Casualties (Partial) 171
D. Honours and Awards 176
E. Some Citations 178
F. Duties of Officers 179
G. Some of the Units Attached as Labour 182

THE 127th BATTALION, C.E.F.
(2nd Battalion, Canadian Railway Troops)

CHAPTER I

IN THE SOMME AREA

When the 12th Regiment, York Rangers, were given the task of raising a battalion of their own for the Canadian Expeditionary Force in November, 1915, to a total of more than 1,100 all ranks, after the 12th had already sent more than twice its peace-time strength to various overseas units, Major F. F. Clarke was sent from his duties in establishing a prisoners of war camp at what became Kapuskasing to take command. The new unit, the 127th Battalion, C.E.F., was recruited from the entire area of York County so Lieut.-Col. Clarke set up local recruiting depots to enlist recruits in their own centres.

The chief recruiting centre, St. Paul's Hall, Yonge Street, also served as Battalion Headquarters, while other depots were localized at Newmarket, Aurora, Sutton, Richmond Hill, King, Markham, Agincourt, North Toronto, Todmorden, West Toronto, Mimico and Woodbridge, and at these centres recruits underwent preliminary training, while Ladies' Auxiliaries were established and branches of the Canadian Red Cross began work in almost every centre. Assistance in the form of funds and equipment came from many sources, including $1,000 towards recruiting costs and equipment from York County Council late in 1915 and another $3,000 early the next year; instruments for the brass band from the Davis Leather Company of Newmarket, and field kitchens provided by the Ladies' Auxiliaries.

Mobilized in Newmarket on 10th April, 1916, after having been brought up to strength, the Battalion marched down Yonge Street to Aurora, where the night was spent, to continue the trek to the new building of the Canadian Kodak

Company then under construction in Mount Dennis. This building bears a bronze tablet with the unit crest and motto recording its first having been used as a barracks by the 127th Battalion, The York Rangers. Then on 13th June, 1916, the unit went under canvas on the common on the west side of Weston Road, an area named Camp Denison, after the well known Canadian military family whose cemetery lies nearby. At the Kodak building, the unit had built sleeping quarters and kitchen and dining equipment, and in its new camp it constructed temporary buildings and put in what equipment was necessary. Services for the camp were supplied locally, Weston extending its water supply free of cost and the Toronto Suburban Railway free electric lighting, while the land was also rent free. The unit used the marquees and mess tents given by the Davis Leather Company.

On 4th August the citizens of Mount Dennis presented the unit with a silver cup of remembrance to "Lieut.-Col. Clarke's Foot Cavalry", a term embodied in the inscription in recognition of the unit's achievements as marching infantry. A fortnight previously, after a march of five miles, the unit won a competition against nine others at Exhibition Camp, Toronto, and was awarded the World Silver Trophy, presented by the publisher of the Toronto newspaper of that name. In July, the unit had entrained for the new Camp Borden, where it spent five weeks of training, before leaving on the 18th by train, embarking on the 21st at Halifax and arriving at Liverpool on the 30th and at Witley camp on the 31st.

Many of the battalions of the C.E.F. were broken up in England, but because of the qualifications of Colonel Clarke and many of his officers and other ranks for engineering and railway construction, the 127th was converted into the new Corps of Canadian Railway Troops. Following their sending a draft to the unit which became the 1st Battalion, C.R.T., the 127th became the 2nd Battalion.

Operations on the Somme caused such serious wastage of manpower that the 127th, warned to be ready to move to Shorncliffe when it became clear it would not be a part of the 5th Canadian Division, was clearly marked for special duties, as 22 of the officers had been engaged in engineering and construction work in civil life and more than 800 of the rank and file had either been railwaymen or had been in construction work. When the Battalion was recruited many men in construction trades had been laid off, and as they were known to Col. Clarke, enlisted in his unit. The 1st Canadian Construction Battalion arriving soon afterwards had many men unfit for service in the field, so the 127th was instructed to supply enough men to that unit to bring it to strength, so that it could leave for France at once. The 127th thus lost two officers and 365 other ranks, including the Regimental Sergeant Major and a Company Sergeant Major. In return the 127th received some 200 reinforcements, who had failed to pass the dental requirements for service in the field, so the men on draft for the 1st Construction Battalion had to be properly treated to go to France if and when the time for such a move arrived. The 1st Canadian Construction Battalion left for France on 26th October, taking a third of the entire strength of the 127th Battalion.

In the interval prior to conversion, the 127th was used principally on instructional staffs. Major Gibson, Lieut. Ritchie and two Sergeants conducted the Engineering School at Witley Camp, where the units in training were taught how to build trenches and erect wire entanglements. Capt. Adams became an instructor at the Bombing School, Capt. Anderson Assistant Staff Captain of the Canadian Division in training, Lieut. H. B. W. Smith divisional instructor in physical training and bayonet fighting, and Lieut. Magee instructor in musketry at Aldershot Training School. Major Craig and Capt. Flood took a three-week course at Chelsea Barracks, London, Lieuts. Clarke, Brunton and Knox a six-week course for officers at Bordon Camp. Lieut. Johnston was Brigade Transport Officer at Witley Camp and eight Sergeants were employed as instructors at the Musketry Camp, Longmoor. The remaining officers and men were employed in building trenches for training purposes on Oakley Common. About 1st November, the unit went to Bramshott Camp, where field training was continued. Conversion to Railway Troops came about mid-month, and on the 25th the unit moved to Bordon, Hants., there to establish a Railway Troops Depot.

Reorganization and outfitting the men for their new role took up the time until 11th January. Reinforcements arriving from the various Training Depots were suitable for railway work, so when the vacancies were filled, a Depot Company was organized under Major Agnew as the nucleus of a new Battalion. Delay took place in securing the proper stores to complete equipping the unit, while new mobilization stores tables had to be provided by the War Office and much equipment peculiar to Railway Troops specially obtained, all of which consumed time. On 11th January the Base Company moved to the new Railroad Headquarters at Purfleet.

By the close of the war, these railway units, serving as Corps and Army Troops, numbered 13 in all, forming a special engineering service for the British Expeditionary Force. The 127th Battalion, therefore, never saw service with the Canadian Corps, and was only with that Corps at Passchendaele when both were serving with the IInd Army.

Destined to see service over the whole extent of the British line in France and Flanders, the 127th operated from the North Sea to the Oise below St. Quentin, save in the Arras-Vimy sector, and was employed with the temporary force which halted the enemy advance at Villers-Brettonneux in his push on Amiens in March, 1918.

Under the command of Lt.-Col. F. F. Clarke, the 127th Battalion, 2nd Canadian Railway Troops, left Bordon Camp, Hants, for Southampton on 11th January, 1917, and there embarked for France the following day in His Majesty's Transport "Mona's Queen", while the mechanical and mule transports sailed in H.M.T. "Sitpah". The mechanical transport consisted of two Sunbeam motor cars, eight Ford box cars and one three-ton truck, in charge of Lieut E. A. Ternan. Disembarking at Le Havre at midnight on the 12th/13th, the unit marched chiefly uphill in a cold rain to Camp No. 1, Sanvic, where no accommodation was available from 4.30 to 7 p.m., then the men found shelter in the Y.M.C.A. huts and in stores buildings. Here steel helmets, gas helmets and tear gas goggles were issued. Two days later the unit entrained for billets in Buire-au-Bois, by way of Neufchatel, Abbéville and Auxi-le-Chateau.

Unit representatives at once drove to Acheux to report to the Assistant Director of Light Railways, Vth Army. An advance party under Major J. M. Gibson, engineering officer, with Lt. Ternan, mechanical engineer officer, Lieut. J. E. Stark, officer in charge of technical stores and 100 rank and file, left for Acheux on the 17th to begin the erection of a base camp to consist of 32 Nissen huts. The party was located in billets at the engineer shops, Varennes, while the work was in progress.

The next day Col. Logan, A.D.L.R.5, conducted a party consisting of Majors Gibson and Swan over the area bounded by Acheux, Beaussart, Colincamps, Sailly-au-Bois and Bertrancourt, where he outlined a programme for building a system of light railway lines. First, a large terminal yard with workshops was to be built at Acheux, from which was to run a main artery to Beaussart, Colincamps and down the Valley north of Sailly-au-Bois towards Hebuterne. Branch lines were to run into Colincamps, Sailly-au-Bois and Mailly Maillet, with a connecting line directly from Beaussart to Courcelles-au-Bois to join another main line running down the Authie Valley from a projected broad gauge railhead at St. Leger. At Sailly-au-Bois this in turn was to connect with the line in the Valley to the north to form a loop. From this connecting line a branch line was to run to the Corps workshops at Bus-les-Artois. From Varennes Royal Engineer Dump a line was to go to Forceville and Englebelmer, this also to be connected to the Acheux Railhead by a direct line and to the main Acheux-Beaussart line by a second from near Forceville to meet it northeast of Acheux Wood.

In the area east of the Ancre another programme was called for in extending and maintaining the system already in existence. This comprised a revision of the line from Aveluy Yard to Donett's Post, eliminating a sinuous heavy grade; construction of a line from the broad gauge railhead at Nab Valley to Nicholl's Loop; a line from Ovillers to the Rifle Dump, and maintenance of the Aveluy-Pozières line.

On the 19th Col. Clarke and survey parties also went to Varennes to start the locations of the proposed light railways in the Vth Army area, and the projected line was reconnoitred from Acheux-Beaussart-Colincamps, to Sailly-au-Bois. At the last two places mentioned, the work was done under shell fire. The proposed line from Beaussart to the Corps workshops at Bus-les-Artois was also located by a survey party under Lieut. D. Graham and the terminal yard at Acheux was surveyed by Capt. A. H. Greenlees. Parties under Lieuts. Ritchie and Lumsden began building a camp at Acheux Yard preparatory to moving the unit from Buire au Bois. Lieut. Emery and a survey party left for Donett's Post as advance party of "D" Company, detailed to take over the system there. Col. Clarke and Major Gibson visited Corps Engineer Headquarters to arrange crossings over the standard gauge railway, and then went to Donett's Post to procure billets for "D" Company, which was to have charge of the work in the Corps area east of the Ancre River. "D" Company arrived at Acheux on the 23rd to a total of 210 all ranks. The next day Battalion Headquarters and the other three companies entrained at Frevent for Doullens, where they marched to billets at Ampliet-Orville. "D" Company arrived at Acheux shortly after midnight, but found no transport to take them to camp as ordered, so marched to Donett's Post beyond Aveluy, arriving that night. Having completed his survey of the proposed line from Beaussart to Colincamps, Sailly-au-Bois and Hebuterne [1], including a spur to a gun position at Courcelles-au-Bois, Lieut. Graham began the location of that from Beaussart to Mailly-Maillet and Auchonvillers on the 25th.

The next day, "D" Company took over the maintenance of the Aveluy-Pozières line; began building a line from the standard gauge railhead in Nab Valley to Nicholl's Loop, and another from Ovillers to the rifle dump past and to the right of Mouquet Farm, where in the previous summer there had been such bitter fighting in the Battles of the Somme. While "A" Company worked on building the camp at Acheux, "B" worked on the Acheux-Beaussart line, grading and laying ties and steel; "C" Company worked on the construction of the Acheux yards with 20-pound rail and "D" built dugouts, engine-houses and completed stables, in addition to the tasks previously mentioned.

---

[1] This line proved particularly difficult, as it was for the most part under direct observation from Gommecourt and the adjoining area, and even this small party was shelled by the enemy.

Some days had been lost in starting the work until authority had been obtained for the appropriation of the Metre Gauge Railway, which at this period was not in use beyond Acheux. Since by so doing, much time and labour was saved, the authority finally came. The line itself was in fairly good condition to Beaussart, except for 3,400 feet near Acheux Wood, where horse traffic had destroyed the grade and the ties had been taken for fire wood, and at a spot where a broad gauge ammunition siding had been extended to cut the line, necessitating a diversion. The ties were showing some signs of decay in the outer shell and about two per cent required replacement. The French practice of slotting the tie to admit the flange of the rail made it necessary before altering to 60-centimetre gauge to adze the ties down to the correct height. The steel was secured to the ties by long bolts and washers, and showed little sign of wear since it was laid. From Beaussart to Aveluy the grade had been appropriated by the broad gauge and the steel and ties thrown to one side, so from that point a new location was necessary. This was completed to Auchonvillers by Lieut. Graham on 9th February.

On 27th January, the unit was given a company of the 20th Cheshire Labour Battalion of about 320 other ranks as labour. These men were all physically unfit and of little use except for very light work. They appeared to have had scant military training and either could not or would not perform any heavy labour. They were also poorly clothed for the inclement weather and complained of insufficient food. The unit, therefore, abandoned any attempt to use them on main line work, and employed them around the Acheux terminal yard for unloading and handling material. On 1st February stock of railway material for construction began arriving and was taken in by Lieut. J. E. Stark, in charge of technical stores.

Meanwhile Lieut. T. W. Clarke began the location of a proposed line from the metre-gauge line at Acheux Wood to connect with the Royal Engineers dump-Englebelmer line, while Major W. G. Swan started changing the gauge of the metre-gauge line to 60 centimetres.

Work on the Ancre Valley line from Aveluy to St. Pierre Divion along the east side of the Ancre River was started by 60 men of "D" Company on 2nd February, while Lieut. Graham finished the location of the line from Beaussart to the Royal Engineers shops at Bus-les-Artois. The next day "D" Company under Capt. Lawrence took over the direction of all light railways in the Corps area in which that Company was located from the 138th A.T. Company, Royal Engineers. In this area the labour supplied to the unit was of a better type, and drawn from the fighting troops in the line. Besides being physically better able to do a good day's work, their experience in the line made them realize the importance of a railway delivering supplies and eliminating much backbreaking labour by carrying parties. One disadvantage, however, consisted in the fact that sometimes Divisions anxious to help detailed a unit for work at 7 a.m., when it had only been relieved the previous night, and on one occasion had only left the front line trenches at 5 a.m. and so the men were worn out for lack of rest. Another drawback was that Brigades did not wish to give one unit all the labour at the expense of training, so detailed alternately among their four battalions, which necessitated sending guides to meet the latter every morning. Not infrequently, they failed to locate the guide or he them until late in the day.

On the 4th the first light railway locomotive of 15 tons was unloaded at Acheux Yard. Col. Clarke and Major Gibson reconnoitred the Aveluy-Mouquet Farm and the Aveluy-St. Pierre Divion lines the following day; saw Brig.-Gen. May at Headquarters, Second Army Corps, to arrange for labour, and were allotted 400 of the Northumberland Fusiliers, who with 20 of "D" Company immediately started construction. Twenty more of "D" Company and 90 of the East Surrey Regiment worked on the Ancre Valley line. By the next day, however, there were employed on the various projects east of the Ancre River: Mouquet Farm-Ovillers line, 410 East Surreys and 26 "D" Company; Ancre Valley line, 200 East Surreys and 33 "D" Company; Tulloch's Dump, 80 East Surreys and 15 "D" Company, and Nicholl's Loop, 150 East Surreys and 20 "D" Company. The following day, Lieut. G. C. Thomas with three non-commissioned officers and 23 sappers of "A" Company were transferred to "D" to assist in building these lines. In addition, other work completed by 9th February included regauging 1.9 miles of track, building 200 feet of sidings and completing 2,000 yards of grading, and the location of the line Beaussart to Auchonvillers was finished. Two days later, "A" Company under Major T. N. Elliott moved to Courcelles-au-Bois to work on the line from Beaussart to Sailly-au-Bois; "B" under Major W. G. Swan to Beaussart, and "C" under Capt. J. H. Craig was detailed to build a spur from Acheux Wood to Bertrancourt dump, in addition to Acheux yard.

The next day the first train moved from Acheux to Beaussart, a distance of 2.3 miles. In addition to the British units mentioned, labour was also provided by the Buffs, the North Hants, the Royal Marine Light Infantry, the Yorkshire and Lancashire Regiment, and the 174th Tunnelling Company, Royal Engineers, at this time. A number of casualties occurred among the infantry from shrapnel on the 15th. All work on the Ancre Valley line was cancelled on this date because the 63rd Division failed to supply enough labour. The forward position of the Ovillers-Mouquet Farm line from Rifle Dump to Zollern and Regina Trenches was reconnoitred. The next day the cancelled work began again with 760 effectives from the 7th Buffs and the Royal Irish Fusiliers. Arrangements were made for the wounded of the 18th (British) Division to be evacuated by way of the line past Mouquet Farm to Rifle Dump. That night a working party repaired track on the Sausage Valley line, damaged by shell fire. Between 4th and 18th February four light railway locomotives, 22 double-truck well cars and 45 single-truck cars had been received and prepared for operation with crews supplied by the unit. On the latter date the Ovillers-Mouquet Farm-Rifle Dump line was completed, and Gen. May of Second Corps expressed his thanks for the task and for the work on the maintenance of the Sausage Valley line.

Instructions were received that the line was to be produced to Desire Trench as soon as possible on the 23rd, and an extension made towards Courcelette of the Aveluy-Pozières line, so construction of both began that day. The next day, however, Lieut. J. McA. Sharp, in charge of the construction of the Courcelette extension, was ordered to cease all work on the Ancre Valley-St. Pierre Divion line and the three miles of track laid and all other moveable material was to be taken to the Courcelette-Desire Trench line and the

Nicholl's Loop extension to Grandecourt. The line to be removed would have been finished in about ten days. Heavy fog came to screen observation by the enemy from Loupart Wood, so Lieut. Sharp's task on the Courcelette line extension was advanced considerably. A reconnaissance of a proposed line from the end of the standard gauge at Colincamps to join a German tramway forward was carried out on the 26th "as far as the enemy permitted", but the line was ordered to be abandoned, and instructions arrived for a survey of an extension of the Beaumont Hamel line to Miraumont by way of Beaucourt-sur-Ancre, with a branch up the ravine towards Pusieux. "D" Company, 4th Battalion, Canadian Railway Troops, relieved "D" Company of the 2nd Battalion on the 27th and took over the work in the area east of the Ancre. Major R. M. Hillary, the medical officer, on the 28th reported four casualties to that date, including one fatal casualty, but that the general health of all ranks was good, despite the fact that the billets occupied for three weeks were unsanitary and several were filthy, while the weather had been unusually severe. The quantity and quality of the rations were satisfactory, although there was a shortage of bread, an important deficiency for a unit employed as this one was. Ordnance and engineering materials were supplied by the Fifth Corps, Vth Army, and the quality of the ordnance was satisfactory, except for field service boots.

Under Capt. A. R. Lawrence, "D" Company moved to a new camp in Tank Valley on 2nd March, while "B" Company was engaged in grading, laying steel and ballasting on the line Mailly-Auchonvillers-Beaumont Hamel with men of the 11th Manchesters and 9th West Yorks. Laying of 40-pound rail was delayed because of the non-delivery of bolts and fish-plates, so it was decided to use 20-pound rails, for which the unit had all the fittings. When it was found impossible to get ⅝-inch bolts for fish-plates, six men made them from ⅝-inch iron.

Night work started on the 3rd and 4th to rush ballast to the line. This ballast was secured from a chalk bank west of Mailly Maillet. A ramp was built with a spur from the main line leading under it. The pit was opened in a long rectangular strip leading to the ramp, which enabled the employment of mules and scrapers. A plough was kept going continuously to loosen the chalk, which enabled a procession of teams following closely to keep a steady stream of ballast flowing through a trap in the floor of the ramp into the trucks below.

"C" Company completed laying track for the Bertrancourt Dump extension line to the ammunition hangers the next day and the track was ready for light traffic the following day. That night "B" Company camp was shelled by German long-range guns firing 6-inch shells. The line along Station road towards Beaucourt and Miraumont was reconnoitred during the day. On the 6th the first train-load of ammunition ran from Bertrancourt Dump to the batteries near Beaumont Hamel, but ballasting on the line at Auchonvillers was interrupted by enemy bombardment.

"D" Company surveyed the Ancre Valley line to Beaucourt and Miraumont; built dugouts and stables for horses and mules and a shop for fitters and the blacksmith and a shelter for the cooks at the new camp site, and were shelled by enemy guns, shrapnel falling within 100 yards of the camp at intervals. The camp of the advance party of "B" Company at Auchonvillers was shelled on the 6th, so it was moved half a mile farther south on Engelbelmer road. That day "B" Company completed location of the line to Beaucourt-sur-Ancre and with parties of the 9th West Yorks and 11th Manchesters ballasted the line Auchonvillers-Beaumont Hamel, and in succeeding days grading and track-laying followed. Three petrol tractors were unloaded and made ready for operation. Enemy shelling and the non-availability of scrapers delayed the work of grading near Beaucourt on the 9th. Col. Clarke, Major Gibson and Lieut. Ternan reconnoitred the proposed line from Beaucourt Station to Beaucourt-sur-Ancre, and the unit was advised that the railhead would be at Auchonvillers in the near future instead of Acheux, so work would soon start on a yard. "C" Company was given charge of the line from Acheux to the Chalk Pit near Mailly-Maillet for completion of ballasting and for maintenance, with parties of the 20th (Labour) Battalion Cheshires and 11th Manchesters. "B" Company was laying track from Auchonvillers to Beaumont Hamel and grading from the latter to Beaucourt. A party of "D" Company was grading from that place to join "B" grading from Beaumont

Hamel. Scrapers arrived on the 10th, but without doubletrees, so material for these was salvaged and blacksmiths put to work making them. On the forward portion of the Beaucourt-Miraumont line, there was more shelling.

An oxy-acetelyne welding plant and a steam pump for washing out engine boilers and filling the water tank from which the engines were supplied were installed on the 11th, when there was some shelling in the Beaumont Hamel area. Building the line past that place, "B" Company had to remove much broken machinery, old rails and other debris, and fill shell holes and craters. The Assistant Director of Light Railways visiting Battalion Headquarters on the 13th announced that future policy in the Army area would be to establish five standard gauge railheads, each about 5,000 yards from the front line, from each of which were to extend two or three light railway lines running as far forward as possible with branches connecting them, thus making a network connection of light railways with the standard gauge railheads. Serre and Miraumont were named as two of the railheads. All efforts of the unit were to be directed towards making the existing line from Acheux Yard and Bertrancourt Dump to Beaucourt ready for steam operation as soon as possible, and to extend this line to a proposed ammunition dump near Miraumont. Because chalk used for ballast was soft, a 15-ton locomotive left the track while hauling a train over a fill near Beaussart that day. The engine fell down the bank and turned over, but the crew escaped without injury and the track was promptly repaired. A section of "B" Company's line from Beaumont Hamel joined "D" Company's section 2,000 feet southeast of Beaumont Hamel corner. The first issue of arms was received by the Battalion, 110 rifles and bayonets, ten per cent of the number required. These arms were to be used to excellent effect later against the enemy.

Brig.-Gen. Benson, G.O.C. Artillery, Fifth Corps, advising Major Gibson that an attack was in preparation at Bucquoy on Sunday, the 18th, and that a daily supply of 128 tons of ammunition was required for the batteries, Major Gibson replied that the line was still under construction, but guaranteed delivery of 50 tons daily. It was, therefore, arranged that the request be complied with; that the operating staff of the formation would be relieved of removing ammunition, and that the operation of the lines would be turned over to the 127th Battalion during the period of preparation for the attack. The unit was also requested to complete the extension of the Beaumont Hamel line to Beaucourt by the 20th for operation of petrol tractors. A request for a train to carry wounded from Mailly to Acheux was met. There was some shelling on that portion of the line towards Miraumont. Another request on the 15th to bring wounded to Acheux from Beaumont Hamel was also satisfied, and 90 tons of ammunition moved over the line from Bertrancourt Dump to Beaumont Hamel. Capt. J. J. O'Gorman, the Battalion veterinary officer, was appointed to take over the veterinary work of the 4th and 3rd Battalions, Canadian Railway Troops, which necessitated visits to their animals at Aveluy Wood, Donett's Post and Albert. Grading from Beaucourt to Miraumont was completed to Station 58, half a mile of construction track was laid and two permanent level crossings were built at Suicide Corner without interruption to traffic. Sleepers were made from fallen timber, culvert material and old standard gauge ties sawn in two. The Battalion was congratulated from General Headquarters for delivering ammunition to the guns within the prescribed time under the most difficult conditions.

Construction of the Beaucourt-Miraumont line by "D" Company towards Baillescourt Farm continued, and a train-load of wounded was brought from Beaumont Hamel to Acheux on the 16th. More ammunition for the guns at Beaumont Hamel was delivered the following day, and three days later as promised the extension from Beaumont Hamel to Beaucourt for the operation of petrol tractors was completed. The next day, however, the Assistant Director of Light Railways ordered that construction cease for the time being, owing to the altered military situation, the enemy having retired from the Ancre Valley area, and warned the unit to be ready to build broad-gauge lines at an early date in the area. Ballasting gangs employed nightly from the first of the month accordingly discontinued work. Then came instructions to use the light railways for moving salvaged ammunition to dumps near standard gauge lines, after which these light lines were to be taken up and moved farther forward. From 21st January to 20th March, some 25¼ miles of light railways had been laid and 23 more miles were surveyed.

Col. Clarke was asked on the 20th to assist in rushing the line from Colincamps to Achiet-le-Grand by grading from the Achiet-le-Grand end, and also to prepare the way for rebuilding the yard there. As soon as the Albert Line reached Achiet-le-Grand to deliver construction material, he was instructed to construct the line from Achiet-le-Grand to Bapaume, including Bapaume Yard and a number of spurs leading from it to proposed ammunition and engineer dumps.

CHAPTER II

BAPAUME OPERATIONS

When Col. Clarke inspected the standard gauge line from Achiet-le-Grand to Bapaume, he found that all rails and 75 per cent of the sleepers had been removed; that German excavations were in railway cuttings for artillery emplacements, but apparently had only been used a short time. Dugouts had been made in the fills, a brick culvert a mile east of Achiet-le-Grand had been blown and there were five large shell holes in the railway formation between Achiet-le-Grand and Bapaume. In Bapaume Yard the rails had been removed, together with switch points, while the frogs had been damaged by explosives, as were six wrecked cars in the yards. The machinery in the railway shops had also been destroyed by explosives applied to the gearing. The overhead bridges at Achiet-le-Grand and Bapaume were both destroyed by explosives and the debris dropped on the railway.

"C" Company under Capt. Craig was instructed to collect ammunition on 21st March and remove track between Auchonvillers Dump and Acheux; to return the ammunition to Bertrancourt Dump, and then take up the track to that dump. "B" Company began removing the debris of the high level steel road-bridge over the railway at Achiet-le-Grand, which task was completed on the 22nd, using dynamite left with fuses and caps by the Germans in an abandoned dugout in the railway embankment. Meanwhile, "D" Company removed track from Beaucourt towards Beaucourt Station. The next day instructions arrived to load for shipment seven locomotives, 35 cars, a petrol tractor and five miles of 20-pound rails with all fittings, while Major Gibson reconnoitred the German lines from Achiet-le-Grand to Mory, to report on the possibility of speedily throwing a light line from a point near Fremicourt to Vaux Vrancourt. Lieut. Sharp with a platoon of "D" Company went to White City to move ammunition to the dump at Suicide Corner, a yard was started in Tank Valley to hold 1,000 tons of ammunition and four miles of light railway track with all sleepers and fittings.

Major Swan with "B" Company began the construction of the formation for a standard gauge line from a junction with the French broad gauge with the Arras-Albert line 1,500 yards north of Miraumont westward towards Pusieux-au-Mont for a distance of 1,000 yards on the 25th. Two dozen high velocity shells burst near the Company's Camp. That day Lieut. R. D. Galbraith and a platoon of "D" Company finished shifting the ammunition to the dump near Auchonvillers and removed 2,200 feet of track there.

The water supply threatened to be the most aggravating of problems in this sector, as all wells were either blown or poisoned, in Achiet-le-Grand the only source of supply being from one well, pumped by a single canvas belt pump. The output of this well was most insufficient to supply a locomotive, so it was necessary when steel arrived here for engines to return to Aveluy for replenishing. Because of the heavy grade from Aveluy to Achiet-le-Grand, much steam was used, so it invariably happened that engines arrived there with just enough water to return to Aveluy. To ensure enough water for locomotives when steel arrived at Bapaume, Col. Clarke instructed Lieuts. Ternan and McIlwraith to investigate sources of supply there. They knew that there must be a well around the Bapaume Yard, but were almost ready to abandon their search, when a well was found in the machine shop. The top had been blown in and all moveable machinery and masonry dumped down the shaft, and a brick wall blasted to cover all trace of it. Work at once began clearing the mouth of the shaft, and erecting a platform and crib to protect it. The heavy hoisting tackle was brought from Battalion Headquarters, and on 1st April after tons of rubble and shattered machine parts of every type had been removed piece by piece, water was found at 75 feet.

On the 26th the unit was equipped with the new pattern small box respirators. Construction now included grading on the standard gauge line from Biefvillers to Bapaume, work on the subway at Achiet-le-Grand, filling the gap in the yard there, grading on the Achiet-le-Grand end of the Colincamps line and ballasting on the Bapaume line. A party moved to the latter centre to begin rebuilding the wrecked railway yard. To the 28th some 500 tons of 6-inch, 8-inch,

60-pounder and 18-pounder shells had been moved to Suicide Corner. A party of "D" Company moved to Avesnes-lez-Bapaume to work on standard gauge construction. An observation balloon breaking from its moorings passed over "B" Company camp on the 30th, breaking the telephone lines and stopping the connection with the railway supply yard at Aveluy for a time.

Col. Clarke went to Headquarters, Vth Army, Albert, on the 31st to a conference at which he undertook to complete the Achiet-le-Grand-Bapaume line by 4th April, with the terminal yard at Bapaume, and also build an extension of about two miles to the Monument Commemoratif by the 7th. The Quartermaster, Capt. E. L. Johnston, reported that day a shortage of 1,324 pounds of bread during the month. On the rations issued, he found it difficult to provide an extra meal at the end of the day, a "sorely needed" addition, as the men worked from 16 to 18 hours daily to meet the demands made upon the unit for construction. Issues of ordnance to replace wornout equipment came forward slowly, and lorries indented for had not yet been received. Lieut. L. F. Johnston, the transport officer, reported that the condition of the mules had improved since the receipt of heavy duty rations, despite the heavy work of preparing railway formation and other labour incidental to railway construction. The occurrence of mud fever caused additional inconvenience because teams were broken up, since the unit had no spare animals. The present animal transport was insufficient, bad roads and long runs making strenuous demands upon it. One of the pair of Sunbeam motor cars was out of commission because spare parts were apparently unobtainable, while the single three-ton lorry was used unsparingly, and the need of eight others, called for in the mobilization stores table, was greatly felt. Ten motorcycles in use were giving good service, but five more were needed. It was also virtually impossible to get motor transport repaired.

On 1st April a survey of the Bapaume Railway Yard was completed, and after water was struck at 75 feet in the well in the wrecked railway shops, repairs on the damaged water tanks continued and a blacksmith's forge was erected. During the day the enemy dropped a number of shells. "B" Company laid 2,300 feet of track in the morning, the line connecting the Colincamps line with Achiet-le-Grand being completed, except for a big fill at Achiet-le-Grand road. "D" Company set up camp at Avesnes-lez-Bapaume the next day under shell fire.

Unit standing orders issued the following day expressed the wish of Col. Clarke that all ranks make themselves thoroughly familiar with all branches of their work; that the unit maintain the name it established as an infantry unit, and never forget the principles laid down then. Each individual was to consider himself an expert in the line of work allotted to him, so that he could be given a party of unskilled labour to work under his direction. All acting non-commissioned officers showing integrity and adaptability would be confirmed in rank on recommendation. The organization was divided into engineering and administrative parts and for better accomplishing the work the company as the unit of work had the same organization.

On 3rd April the first locomotive entered Bapaume Yard at 10 p.m., thus establishing connection a day ahead of the time requested by Gen. Gough, Commanding Vth Army, and instructions were received to locate a light railway line from the Monument Commemoratif to Vaux Vrancourt. The following afternoon an enemy aircraft shot down two observation balloons along the unit line. The first engine in Bapaume Yard was supplied with water the next day, when an oxy-acetelyne plant was installed and the steel rails at the Arras road crossing were cut. A high velocity shell fell in the gasworks about 100 yards from the well, killing six men and 16 horses on the 6th. "B" Company completed six sidings at and near Bapaume, and the grading of the line connecting Colincamps extension with Achiet-le-Grand was completed. Construction of the line from Bapaume to the Monument Commemoratif began, and on the 8th the first ammunition train arrived in Bapaume.

Steel was laid on the line to the Monument with the labour of the 30th Battalion, Australians, the following day, when the Grevillers and Avesnes spurs were completed. Instructions were received the next day to extend the line from Bapaume to Velu and to abandon the line from the Monument to Vaux Vrancourt. "D" Company camp area was shelled intermittently, but no damage was done. An average daily shipment of 20 cars of light railway materials to Achiet-le-Grand, the new railhead, and also to Fremicourt, was made from the first of the month to date. After a party consisting of one sergeant and 35 men of "B" Company was sent to the 4th Battalion, Canadian Railway Troops, to assist in filling a crater 60 feet wide and 20 feet deep made by a mine explosion on the line north of Achiet-le-Grand Yard on the 12th, the track was ready again for traffic before midnight. The next day Sgt. F. Bingham of "B" Company discovered a mine in the railway formation 50 feet west of the Cambrai road crossing near Fremicourt, containing 36 packages of "Perdit" connected with a detonator, fuse and a pair of lead wires, evidently to be fired by an electric battery. Since construction began from Achiet-le-Grand, Sgt. Bingham had found mines from which more than 1,000 pounds of "Perdit" had been taken. That day a locomotive, derailed about half-way between Fremicourt and Bapaume, was replaced on the track.

Enemy high velocity guns shelled Avesnes-lez-Bapaume heavily on the 14th, one shell striking the unit's construction locomotive, blowing a hole in the boiler and destroying the track under the wheels. Spr. N. Nicholson was badly scalded and sent to hospital. A mine under the track a mile north of Achiet-le-Grand towards Arras exploded the previous night, making a crater 35 feet deep and 80 feet across. Enemy shelling upset "D" Company camp, but did no damage that day and the next, when little progress could be made in construction and maintenance, as no labour was available from the Australian units, which were standing to with machine guns along the new trenches behind the German entanglements near Battalion Headquarters and "A" and "C" Company Camps the previous night. The railway yard and its vicinity were shelled during the day and on the next, but the 2nd Battalion, Canadian Railway Troops, had no casualties. "D" Company located a new camp at Lebucquière, and 175 other ranks were employed on construction, the work divided into preparing railway formation, bridge building, salvaging steel and timber and in surveying. Reconstruction of the wrecked railway bridge over the road between Lebucquière and Velu began, the camp being under shell fire. Spr. H.R. Wagstaffe was wounded by shrapnel while driving the water cart.

In three days "A" Company laid 7,400 feet of track east of Bapaume towards Fremicourt, the line to the latter being completed on the 18th, when Velu Station was blown up by a mine, which killed 10 and injured 26 Australian other ranks, also injuring Sprs. W. Harris and W.A. Westbeare of "D" Company. Shelling continued almost daily, one of the shells in the yard on the 20th from an enemy high velocity gun exploding at Station 18, blowing a crater 18 feet wide and 14 deep, the sixth to be made in the yard. Fortunately, however, many of the shells were "duds". The following day Major Gibson located two spurs east of Velu for two 12-inch howitzers 500 yards apart, in positions from which their flashes would be masked. A gas alarm sounded twice that day. When Col. Clarke inspected the line from Achiet-le-Grand to Fremicourt on the 23rd, he found the line from the former to Bapaume in first-class condition, and ready to be turned over to maintenance, this being done the next day. Track laying to the first Beugny crater was completed by Lieut. A.G. Bonn and a party of "B" Company, while Lieut. H.B. Lumsden and another party filled two craters east of Beugny. Eight three-ton lorries arrived the following day to complete establishment, but three were not new, having been commandeered at the beginning of the war. A large marquee containing stores was burned, but there was no material damage beyond the loss of the marquee. The cause was probably spontaneous combustion among cotton waste.

Three bents of a pile bridge 124 feet long to replace one destroyed by the enemy were driven that night. The next day enemy shelling was resumed, and on the 27th enemy shells fell in Bapaume Yard, killing ten men and five horses and damaging four lorries and two waggons, all belonging to the Australians. The pile bridge was ready for crossing at 5 p.m. that day. Col. Clarke and Capt. A.H. Greenlees reconnoitred the area east of Hermies the next day with a view to extending the line from Velu across the Canal du Nord. Fremicourt Yard was shelled by a high velocity gun and howitzers. A party worked until midnight on the 29th clearing the main line and siding, where formerly was the German railway yard, a spot now known as Summit Yard, for the night before an engine pushing a car of steel collided with a derailed tractor there and blocked the line.

The next day a train of railway material ran from Fremicourt to Summit Yard for distribution along the line and steel was laid into Velu at noon, about 9.3 miles from Achiet-le-Grand. The Summit Yard area was heavily shelled during the day. About 150 of "D" Company were engaged in track laying and ten on the bridge, with 200 of the 11th and 12th Australian Battalions as labour. Since the 15th, this Company had laid some 8,300 feet of track; 1,800 feet of siding; put on two switches, and also completed four miles of formation. The bridge over the Velu road was made of salvaged material, the bolts and nuts being made in the Company's blacksmith's shop, and the wheelbarrows by their mechanics. Siding 1,100 feet long in Fremicourt Yard was completed by "B" Company. Since the 18th Lieut. J.E. Stark and his staff with parties of German prisoners had been collecting salvaged ammunition and light railway material left at dumps along the railway in the Auchonvillers-Beaumont Hamel area. That night the Summit Yard area was heavily shelled.

On 1st May Major Gibson carried out the location of two spurs east of Chateau Wood, Velu, for two 12-inch howitzers mounted on railway trucks, and grading of these spurs began. Col. Clarke was instructed to survey three alternative schemes for future extension of the main line towards Marcoing, eliminating the high level railway bridge over the Canal du Nord, destroyed by the enemy on his retirement. Col. Clarke was also to proceed with the construction of a line from Velu to Ytres on which were four large craters, two to be filled, a third to be spanned by a frame bridge and a fourth by a pile bridge 140 feet in length. The last mentioned bridge and the line for a mile south of it would be hard to build rapidly, as they were under direct enemy observation. Any movement was followed by hostile shelling, so work would have to be carried on at night, without lights and as noiselessly as possible. The crater at Beugny Bridge was being filled by a party using horse scrapers and wheelbarrows.

When the enemy shelled Fremicourt Yard the next day, two trucks loaded with ammunition were damaged and one of the Australian working party was killed. The bridge built over the crater near Beugny was also shelled and a pile was blown. Organized field sports at the "C" Company camp were held, the first relaxation the men had had since their arrival in France, while the work continued on the gun spurs and 25 cars of light railway material was collected from Acheux Yard and the dumps at Auchonvillers, Mailly-Maillet and Beaussart for the Anzac Light Railways. Enemy shell fire continued throughout the day. A start was made in locating the proposed lines from Velu to the Canal du Nord the following day, while progress was made in building the spurs in Velu Wood for the railway-mounted howitzers and the carpenters built emplacements for them. On the 4th the line at the crossing of the Anzac Light Railway on the Cambrai road was blocked for four hours because of a collision of one of the 2nd Battalion's construction trains with a tractor and ammunition train crossing the diamond without lights, but was cleared by one of the wrecking crews of the Battalion. At Fremicourt the line was broken for an hour by shelling.

That night two 12-inch howitzers were hauled by a train in charge of Col. Clarke to Velu Wood and placed on the spurs there. Bapaume Yard was bombed by an enemy aircraft about 9 p.m., but no damage was done. A new camp at Ytres was set up for "A" Company, and the Company's work in the Velu area, totalling 11,850 feet, was completed. A party of "C" Company had to be removed from Velu because the line was shelled steadily, while a new company camp site near Bertincourt station was selected. The next day "B" Company surveyed a proposed new hospital spur south of Beugny. Between 9 p.m. and midnight an air battle took place over the Company camp. In charge of despatching and operating construction trains, Lieut. A.H. McIlwraith since 1st May had daily forwarded material for construction and ballasting of the line to Velu and handled 368 cars of freight; 159 of ammunition, 124 of stone for roads, 52 of light railway material, 27 of sleepers, two of coal, two of telegraph line material and two special trucks mounting two 12-inch howitzers. On the morning of the 5th, an ammunition train was shelled in Fremicourt Yards, two cars being damaged. Owing to continuous shelling of these yards, operations were carried on chiefly at night. An aircraft raid over the yards the next day caused no damage, the men taking shelter from the bullets. An enemy aircraft flew low over the Battalion Headquarters camp at 1.30 the following morning; was fired at from the camp by machine guns, and dropped three bombs between it and Fremicourt Yard without casualties or damage. The Yard was shelled that day from 7 a.m. until the evening. "C" Company's camp was shelled that evening, but the personnel took shelter in dugouts.

Lieut. Ternan, the mechanical engineer officer, moved from Bapaume to Velu Junction to start the installation of water supply. At Bapaume he had repaired two 15,000-gallon tanks and raised them 12 feet from the ground on a timber structure; deepened the well in the railway shops there about 90 feet by the removal of more broken machinery, bricks and other debris, and erected a stand-pipe in the well and connected with the tanks. At Velu he set an upright for repairing a 10,000-gallon steel tank, which formerly stood by the well. It had been shot through in many places and needed much repairing. Water was found in the well 105 feet below ground level. The top of the well was badly damaged and because of debris, the water was only 2 feet 6 inches deep in the clear. A workshop was built to carry out repairs. "A" Company was using mule transport to remove the debris from a blown brick bridge on the line near Ytres to make way for a timber trestle bridge, the debris being used to fill two craters in the formation near Ytres Station. While work was continued by "B" Company in Fremicourt Yard, a party of "C" Company completed a siding near Bertincourt and the remainder of the company pushed on with the work in Bapaume Yard under the supervision of Capt. Craig. A party of "D" Company under Lieut. Sharp continued operations on the main line at Velu and another under Lieut.

Brunton in Velu Station Yard under enemy shell fire all day, while Lieut. Stark loaded four cars with timber and light railway material at Acheux. Fremicourt Yard continued to be shelled almost daily, and on the night of the 9th parties of "B" Company there had to leave work because of it, despite which the lifting of the main siding was completed.

Velu Yard parties of "D" Company tracklaying for the cross-over for the Velu-Ytres lines were shelled on the 10th, and there were seven casualties, but only one had to be sent to a clearing station, and work was resumed promptly. Heavy shelling at Velu that morning interrupted the work of Lieut. Ternan and his party, but in the afternoon a pump was installed in the well and the first locomotive was supplied with water that night. Preparations were made the next day for the construction of the pile bridge over the crater on the line from Velu to Ytres, piles being driven by a pile driver. Progress would determine how soon construction of the bridge and the continued construction of the line towards Ytres would begin. In the vicinity of the bridge, 140 shells were dropped that day, slightly damaging the line. That night an enemy barrage made work near the pile bridge and the crater impossible.

CHAPTER III

THE FIFTH ARMY AREA AND THE SAND DUNES

For the week ended 12th May, a survey had been made of the Ytres-Etricourt Station Yard and the plans forwarded, besides a survey of the line between Ytres Station and Bertincourt, with a spur running off to the right, the site of an enemy ammunition dump. This spur was located as far as the Ytres-Bertincourt Road Crossing. A total of 11,500 feet of formation had been prepared without any allocation of labour, the IVth Army advising that no troops were available for the purpose. "B" Company started work on Fremicourt Yard, breakfasting at 5.30 and working until 12.30 p.m. The yard siding in Bapaume Yard was completed. "B" and "D" companies spent the 13th in field sports at "B's" camp, with the Battalion Band in attendance. An enemy shell struck the football field at the end of the game, but there were no casualties. Instructions were received the next day to discontinue construction of the bridge on the line at Ytres, as the Royal Engineers complained that their progress in building north to meet the Canadians at the boundary of the IVth Army area was delayed by the work on the bridge. The bents of the latter were, however, in place and ready for stringers and decking. The unit had cleaned off the old formation from the south end of Ytres Yard to this bridge and prepared the formation ready for tracklaying. The proposed extension towards Marcoing was surveyed.

On the 15th a locomotive used for hauling the pile driver to and from the crater to a covered position in a deep cutting was suddenly derailed through the settlement of the track over what may have been a destroyed enemy dugout. As a result, the pile driver had to be moved by manpower with the help of an auxiliary engine on the plant. As a fog settled, it was possible to continue driving piles at 6 p.m., two hours after the engine was derailed, and as rain and fog continued all night, the next day and for several succeeding days, this enabled pile driving to be completed in the afternoon, and by 6.30 p.m. the deck placed. "C" Company then laid 1,900 feet of track by 11.30 p.m., followed by a track laying party of "A", who laid 1,333 feet by 5.20 a.m. the next morning. Rain and fog in the night made the task very unpleasant, but it screened the light of the lanterns from enemy observation in Havrencourt. "A" Company was followed by "D", who laid 3,480 feet by noon.

South of Bertincourt the work was held up and between two and three hours was lost through the fog suddenly lifting. When the enemy saw the locomotives and the steel train, he promptly shelled it, forcing the train to move into the cover of a deep cut at Bertincourt. At noon "B" Company taking over the work laid 1,950 feet by 6 p.m. The steel train's inability to close up on the track laying party caused a long haul by hand lorry from the cut to the work, and so hampered progress. At 6 p.m., "A" Company took over and laid 3,346 feet to the point at which they met the end of steel from the south on the 18th, which made a total of 12,069 feet laid in this operation. Grading on this line was done entirely by the unit, as IVth Army grading parties had not arrived.

On the 17th, General Sir Hubert Gough, General Officer Commanding the Vth Army, with members of his staff and some French officers, accompanied by Col. Clarke, inspected the line from Achiet-le-Grand to Velu, travelling by special train. Lieut. Ternan and his party continued repair work at Velu Station and also began deepening the well on the 18th. That evening heavy shelling made it necessary to leave camp temporarily. The next day Fremicourt Yard generally was shelled, forcing "B" Company parties to disperse. A party of "C" Company with 22 mules and scrapers preparing formation in a cutting and filling a crater under a bridge was shelled, as was the Company Camp, but there were no casualties, although a tent and some camp equipment were lost. The following day the Battalion was visited by Lt.-Col. the Hon. Angus Macdonell, assistant director, Railway Troops; Major Thomas A.H. Taylor, Staff Captain, Headquarters, Canadian Railway Troops; Capt. Walter Curran, Canadian War Records Office, and F.A. McKenzie and John Kidman, Canadian Press correspondents.

By order of General Gough an expression of his appreciation was forwarded to the unit on the 24th, on the work done by the Battalion on the construction of broad gauge lines in the Vth Army area, commending the unit for what he called the speed and efficiency shown. The day was devoted to sports and athletic competitions. With the brass and bugle bands, the companies met at "B" Company camp and marched to Battalion Headquarters between Fremicourt and Bapaume under Col. Clarke and Major T.H. Holdsworth, second-in-command. For the encouragement of commendable rivalry among the Companies and Headquarters, prizes were awarded for the best appearing waggon drawn by four mules and in charge of two drivers and attended by two cooks. Following the races and competitions in the afternoon, a concert was given in the evening, after which "A", "C" and "D" Companies were returned to their camps by special train. Instructions were received that day to take over the light railways in the Vth Army area from the 4th Battalion, Canadian Railway Troops, as well as to complete the broad gauge work in hand. (1) This work consisted of completing the yard at Achiet-le-Grand; the line thence to a junction with the trench tramways by way of Mory, with a branch line to Ecoust St. Main; the main line from Delville Wood to Perth Siding, and the yard at Bapaume, to be known as Hun Dump. Branch lines from Bapaume to the Monument Commemoratif, from Fremicourt by way of Vaux, from Beugny to Maricourt Wood and from Anzac Junction to Beaumetz-les-Cambrai, were also to be completed.

Lieut. A.H. McIlwraith turned over to Ordnance three standard gauge locomotives and one petrol tractor on the 26th, and 13 locomotive engineers and firemen of the Battalion were sent to Audricq by order of Headquarters, Canadian Railway Troops. A total of 22 had previously been despatched. Major Swan left for Belgium as one of a number of officers of various units sent to assist in pre-

---

(1) From 28th March to 31st May lines completed, including sidings, totalled 24.7 miles; lines graded or cleared, 27.2 miles; lines surveyed 31.4 miles, and bridges built three.

paring for the Messines offensive. Light railway construction and maintenance had just got under way by the 29th, when orders arrived for the despatch of Battalion Headquarters and "A" and "B" Companies to Belgium under IInd Army. It was, therefore, necessary for the remaining two Companies to assume the entire responsibility for the whole system in the Bapaume area. Simultaneously, instructions called for a survey party to perform special work in the south of France, so Lieut. T.W. Clarke and 11 other ranks of "C" Company were detailed, leaving by lorry that day for Trouville. This party arrived at their destination on the 31st, and were told that their line started at Tourqueville, locating a camp centrally the following day at Touques. A French lady provided Lieut. Clarke with the use of a sun room for drafting. The next day the party began location work, completing it on 4th June to a rest camp and hospital site. On the 6th instructions were received to go to the Forêt de Brotonne, where camp was pitched the next day near No. 16 Prisoners of War Headquarters on the Seine. Surveys began on the proposed lines at Mailleraye to Le Vuy Mills and a forest extension to Pine Copse. Great care was necessary to avoid trees on private property, which slowed the work. On 7th July these surveys were completed, and the party rejoined their Company on the 10th at Oost Dunkerque.

In the Bapaume area, "C" and "D" Companies came under the Assistant Director of Light Railways, and with slight alterations continued the work outlined above on taking over from the 4th Canadian Railway Troops. Headquarters and "A" and "B" Companies were ordered to entrain to join the IInd Army on 2nd June. On the morning of the 1st, Bapaume Yard was shelled by large calibre guns and two light railway switches were blown, but the damage was repaired at noon. The work on the Velu-Ytres line was completed that day, a task done hastily because of the morrow's move, only the most urgent places being worked with a view to maintenance parties filling in and ditching. The horse transport under Lieuts. L.F. Johnston and J.T. Jenkins, consisting of 25 waggons and 102 animals, including saddle horses, took the Arras Road through Bapaume in the morning, making a steady rate of about five kilometres an hour. Camp was made for the night in a large field between Arras and Mont St. Eloy. Back at Velu, Lieut. Ternan continued repairing the water tank in the Yard until 9 a.m., when heavy shelling occurred, continuing until 4 p.m., in which interval some 500 shells were dropped without damage either to yard or to water supply.

Headquarters and "A" and "B" Companies entrained at noon the next day under Major Holdsworth with 13 officers and 450 other ranks. At Poperinghe Yard early the next morning, the train was held up by heavy shelling of the town by high velocity guns, and when the shelling moved near the location of the train at 8 a.m., it ran into the yard. The horse transport reached Bethune that afternoon, and Col. Clarke, with the mechanical transport arrived at 8 p.m.

"C" and "D" Companies meanwhile continued with the work allotted in the Bapaume area until the 18th, when acting on instructions from Col. Clarke, "D" Company marched from Velu to Bapaume, where it joined "C" and both entrained at 11 a.m. for an unknown destination in Belgium, "D" under Major Lawrence and "C" under Capt. Greenlees. The transport section of "C" left Bapaume in the morning for Battalion Headquarters near Poperinghe. The following day Capt. Craig with Capts. Johnston and Emra went to Dunkerque to visit Fifteenth Corps Headquarters, where they found that "C" and "D" Companies were to be located at Coxyde in the IVth Army area. "C" arrived at the camp site selected at 1.45 p.m. on the 20th and "D" at Coxyde-les-Bains at 2.30 p.m. to spend the night in French huts. The following morning "D" pitched tents on the sand dunes. On the 21st, "C" shifted to Oost-Dunkerque Bains, taking a well-sheltered location in the dunes just south and west of the crossroads.

"C" Company assumed the maintenance of the 60-centimetre system east of the road from Oost-Dunkerque to Oost-Dunkerque Bains and north of the road from Oost-Dunkerque Bains at right angles to the Nieuport Canal. In the latter part of the month the work of maintenance and construction in this area was started and carried on without casualties. The area had just been taken over by the British from the French and few enemy guns were concentrated here prior to 1st July. With a party of "C" Company, Lieut. Draper on the morning of 2nd July was, however, hampered by enemy shell fire in construction work through the dunes and in the afternoon was forced to stop. Lieut. A.R. Clarke with another party of that Company was building a gun spur through the dunes, when two enemy shells exploded at 2 p.m. on the grade as a section was leaving for lunch, Cpl. J. Rushworth being killed, Spr. D.J. Dillon mortally wounded and seven other Sappers wounded. In the morning two shells alighted in the camp area, killing one man and wounding two others belonging to neighbouring units. Lieut. Clarke and Cpl. Day speedily cared for the wounded.

With two parties of "C" Company the following day, Lieut. A.O.L. Cameron was employed in grading, while a portion of his men prepared the track and switches on the line paralleling the Shore road. Lieut. Clarke continued the work on the gun spur, grading 250 feet, while Lieut. Gordon laid 1,200 feet of steel and ballasted 900 feet on the line through the sand dunes. The Battalion Chaplain visited the camp and early that afternoon held a short memorial service.

On the 4th, Lieut. Gordon's party found it necessary to take shelter from enemy shrapnel while working on the construction. That day Lieut. Draper's parties revetted the cuttings through the sand, using canvas and wire netting. Lieut. A.R. Clarke continued with the grading on the gun spur, completing 450 feet, while the maintenance parties during the day filled 14 shell holes, prepared grade and laid new steel in 16 places. Capt. Craig, commanding "C" Company, visited all the lines that day, while Capt. Greenlees, the second-in-command, worked on a survey in the Abbécappelle sector south of Oost-Dunkerque. Heavy shell fire during the day made it necessary to repair 450 feet of track, which was accomplished so as not to delay night traffic. Cpl. Rushworth and Spr. Dillon were buried in the military cemetery at Coxyde, Capt. Allan, the Chaplain, officiating.

Lieut. Gordon's party was delayed an hour and a half the following day by shell fire, and Lieut. Cameron's parties were compelled to relinquish their tasks for a short time. On the 7th the tool box of Lieut. Gordon's party was hit by a shell, causing a good deal of loss and damage to the tools. Capt. Craig arranged with the "Q" Staff in Dunkerque for trench rations for the company while engaged in night work. Sgt. Weeks worked with a party from 1 p.m. until 9 p.m. replacing rails broken by shell fire. Throughout the day heavy enemy shelling greatly interfered with the work of all parties, necessitating much maintenance work owing to breaks in the track. Because of the failure of the operating company on the 9th to supply pioneer trains as arranged, work was held up for all parties, the chief shortage being 50-metre curb rails and wooden ties. The following morning parties went to work as usual, Capt. Greenlees proceeding to stake out a siding. He had just reached the site when the enemy opened a most intense bombardment of the whole area, which not only affected all working parties, but the entire shore sector for a distance of seven miles back of the line. When it was possible to do so, the parties were marched back to camp by their officers. Increasing in violence, the bombardment continued all that day, a terrific barrage sweeping the rearward area for miles. Two men of Lieut. Clarke's party were slightly gassed and he himself hit in the right arm by a heavy piece of shrapnel. While still in the gassed area under shell fire, Cpl. G.E. Day[2] rendered first aid to the wounded officer.

Capt. Greenlees had probably the most unsavoury experience that day, as he was caught in the barrage and forced to lie for an hour and a half in a shell hole in water to his neck. As a result he later suffered a severe illness. Seeing the intensity of the barrage over the forward area, the Company Commander tried to reach the shore party, but met a member of it returning, who informed him that instructions had been followed, and the parties had been divided into small sections, which had either taken cover or were finding their way back to camp through the sheltering sand hummocks. Once the whole company

---

(2) He received the Military Medal, and died 9th May, 1918.

was back in camp, all ranks sheltered in two large dugouts in the camp area. This bombardment proved to be one of the worst of the war, and under it the enemy advanced to the east bank of the Nieuport Canal, within 400 yards of the line the Company was maintaining.

Continuing throughout the night of the 10th/11th, the bombardment died away towards morning. The Company's maintenance patrols found a mile and a half of track paralleling the road from Oost-Dunkerque to the Canal blown out, so the two companies of attached infantry were ordered to be ready for work on the line. All of the Company available went to the site of the most serious damage and by 6 p.m. had filled all shell holes and rebuilt the mile and a half of track destroyed, so by that night normal traffic was resumed. The road parallel to this piece of track was filled with huge shell holes and all traffic on it effectually blocked by waggons and artillery limbers driven into the holes in the night. For three days no effort was made to repair it, so the light railway was the only available means of transport for ammunition for the forward batteries. During the day parties had to leave their work on one section of the line because of heavy shell fire. Capt. Greenlees superintended the work of rebuilding the shore line, where also a large portion had to be replaced.

Lieut. Gordon and two parties of "C" Company and attached parties of the 2nd/7th Lancashire Fusiliers were employed on the 12th assembling steel and in track laying to the end of the gun spur, also completing 600 feet of grading. Similar parties under Lieut. Draper also graded and laid track, hampered by enemy shell fire. The work continued the following day, again under shell fire. Day and night parties patrolled all lines, repairing all breaks caused by shell fire. The next day Lieut. Cameron with a party of "C" Company and some Lancashire Fusiliers completed building the line through the sand dunes, a task which had entailed very heavy work in grading, cuts and fills of eight to ten feet being common. Mules with slush scrapers were used when possible for this work, some of which was performed at night to avoid direct observation. Lieut. Clarke's party graded 2,200 feet on the proposed line a mile long parallel to the Canal and a mile to the west. Because of more shell fire, the work of assembling the steel was suspended for about an hour. Capt. Greenlees meanwhile began location for the proposed line to the batteries in the area of Spellerek. Night maintenance parties under Lieut. Draper patrolled the forward system.

Lieut. Gordon and parties of "C" Company and the Lancashire Fusiliers were engaged in building a new spur to a Royal Engineers dump on the 15th, after Lieut. T.W. Clarke had placed grade stakes with a survey party that morning. On the following day, Lieut. Gordon and a party put in a switch and graded on the gun spur, while Lieut. Draper and a party lifted and lined 3,800 feet of track and Lieut. T.W. Clarke's survey party put in stakes for the gun spur and another spur. The maintenance parties repaired the line in several places where it had been broken by shell fire. The Lancashire Fusiliers had now been withdrawn, and no labour reported that day. It was the endeavour of the Canadians in this area to cooperate in every way with the Battery Commanders, and wherever possible to supply gun spurs for the delivery of ammunition by rail. Fortunately, considerable latitude was allowed by the Assistant Director of Light Railways in making recommendations for work of this kind, and as a result necessary work could frequently be completed without undue delay. Artillery caterpillars crossing sections of track sometimes created difficulties, but they were gradually eliminated by keeping close touch with Battery Commanders.

Arrangements were made with Major George, son of Prime Minister Lloyd George, commanding the Naval Battery, on the 20th to notify the Canadians when guns were to be taken in or out of the battery positions so that steps could be taken to protect the track. That day Spr. G.A. Fitzgerald was wounded by shrapnel. Two days later parties under Lieut. T.W. Clarke worked on general maintenance, and because the track was badly shelled, it was necessary to work until 10 p.m. to finish the task. The next day the work of building a gun spur to some 18-pounder batteries had to be abandoned because of enemy shell fire, Sprs. S.T. Wolfe and R.M. Skinner being wounded. On the evening of the 27th instructions were received to make every effort during the night to facilitate delivery of ammunition over all lines under the company's maintenance. As a result, it was necessary to employ men who had been working all day in shifts under the officers, but there was no delay. The next day 22 sections of steel blown out by enemy fire at noon had to be replaced, but traffic was resumed at 4 p.m., all repairs having been made.

At night Lieut. T.W. Clarke with a party of "C" Company and the 154th Labour Company graded and laid steel on a spur to the Swift Shore Battery. Heavy bombardment by enemy gas shells forced the discontinuance of the work at midnight. Lieut. Cameron with a night maintenance party continued ballasting and general maintenance. His party also encountered gas shells, Spr. W.B. Smith having to be removed to hospital badly gassed. Lieut. Draper and two parties of "C" and of the 154th Labour Company working on the extension of a spur also had to stop at about that time because of a heavy bombardment of gas and high explosive shells. Spr. A. Bigras was killed and Lieut. Draper wounded in the left arm, and the Officer Commanding the Labour Company in the hip. Several of the Labour and "C" Company men were gassed. After the various night parties returned, it was discovered that four were unaccounted for, so Capt. Craig, Cpl. Ross and Spr. Draper made a search through the gassed area, returning at dawn with two of the Labour men in a dazed condition. The four missing men reported later. Ultimately a number of very bad cases developed from those exposed this night.

During the month, 15 miles of track were located; eight miles laid, ballasted and completed, and an average of ten miles was maintained. A daily average of 90 all ranks of "C" Company were employed on construction, and 85 on maintenance, besides attached labour, within three miles of the enemy trenches. Most of the construction work was done within two miles of the line. On 7th August, "C" Company moved to Coxyde, there to entrain for Bergues, where it was to work on standard gauge track. During the month 39 casualties resulted from enemy action, a large number of which were the results of the new mustard gas, the properties of which were not then known.

For two weeks Lieut. Cameron was in charge of forward maintenance and was awarded the Military Cross for the leadership and devotion to duty he displayed in maintaining the lines under fire, and specifically for his gallantry on 30th July west of Nieuport, when the crossroads were heavily shelled by large calibre and high explosive shells. His party twice relaid a section of track which was blown out a third time by enemy shell fire, while the party was at work on the adjoining section. The party took refuge in a covered way to the trenches, when the covered way was blown in at either end and also in the midst of the party. Work during the period involved patrolling tracks 24 hours a day. All lines were kept in repair for operation to the gun emplacements, despite a heavy bombardment with mustard gas and high explosive shells. Nineteen of the party of 22 in a dugout became casualties from shell fire or from mustard gas and one of the remaining three was later incapacitated for duty. Although suffering from gas poisoning, Lieut. Cameron remained on duty.

"C" and "D" Companies detrained at Bergues at 6 a.m. on 8th August and pitched camp. On the main line from Dunkerque to Proven, each company was allotted for maintenance about 4,500 feet of double track, which was in very bad condition and needing to be lifted, ballasted with from four to eight inches of mine earth ballast and surfaced. Part of the line was laid in a very wet, spongy section, and as it was low, great care had to be exercised to drain it properly. "C" Company's section extended 1,400 yards eastward from Bergues Exchange, so the next day parties cleared sand from between ties for 2,500 feet of track, preparing for lifting and reballasting, and completing 300 feet of ditching and inserting new fish plates where necessary. To assist in the work 150 of the 134th Labour Company were attached. The following day "C" Company was also given the task of maintaining 6,500 feet of track west of Cassell road. Daily trainloads of mine earth were supplied.

When taken over the yard throughout was in extremely poor condition, the sand ballast having been washed from under the ties by the heavy rain. No effort had been made to keep open the drainage system, which at best was inadequate for the work of draining the low section in which the yard had been built. Before the arrival of the Canadians, trains were continually being derailed, and even a few days of work reduced the number of derailments. Capt. Greenlees went to hospital on the 18th. The next day "C" Company undertook to supply data to the survey section for the preparation of a proper drainage system for the whole of the Bergues Yards, so on succeeding days the survey party took levels, traversing the yard for the preparation of a plan. On the 23rd, IVth Army routine orders published the award of the Military Medal for bravery under fire to Cpl. G.E. Day.

During the stay of the Company at Bergues, several visits were received from Major Holdsworth; the medical officer, Lt.-Col. Hillary; Capt. Marshall, and the Chaplain, Capt. Allan, who held several services. Major Craig was promoted to the rank of major, effective 13th January, 1917. A total of 13.8 miles of yard track was traversed for the preparation of the map mentioned, .38 miles of grade was constructed, 2.85 miles of grade prepared and 2.85 miles of track was ballasted and surfaced. Instructions were received that the work of collecting and plotting data for the map was to be handed over to the 5th Battalion, Canadian Railway Troops, which was done on 28th August. The next day the Company left to rejoin the Battalion in the Ypres Salient after a short stay at a rest camp at Watou.

CHAPTER IV

THE MESSINES OFFENSIVE

After arrival at Poperinghe early on 3rd June and their final location in camp at the rear of Steentge Windmill, where they were joined at noon by the mechanical transport from Bapaume by road, Headquarters and "A" and "B" Companies of the Battalion learned that they were to assume responsibility for the work of the 7th Battalion, Canadian Railway Troops, who had suffered heavy casualties at Ypres. On the 5th, the Battalion, therefore, took over the line to a point known as "White Pole Corner", two lines to the village of St. Jean and four others in that sector. Major Lumsden of the 4th Battalion, Canadian Railway Troops, acting temporarily as Light Railway Staff Officer, was sent to help the unit get in touch with the work. When Capt. Anderson and Lieut. Graham inspected the lines mentioned, they found all under constant bombardment by high explosive and gas shells, while at some points forward of Ypres they were swept periodically by machine gun fire. The lines in Ypres promised to be particularly difficult owing to flying brick from shattered buildings.

As the work for the preparation for the offensive at Messines was very trying, reliefs every few days were arranged, "A" Company taking the first on 5th June, with quarters in dugouts of elephant iron and sandbag construction on the east slope of a stream parallel to the Yser Canal, screened from air observation by trees and heavy foliage. As labour the Battalion took over the 16th Battalion, Rifle Brigade, billeted in Ypres. Most of the construction work had to be done at night, and in the next few days strong maintenance parties were kept constantly on the lines to keep open communication to the Batteries supporting the attack. Another line was taken over by the Battalion the following day.

Work in Ypres began by ballasting from White Pole Corner to the bridge over the Yser Canal, enemy shelling making it necessary to move the working parties from place to place. His bombardments were concentrated and continuous on certain points, after which they ceased suddenly to resume elsewhere. When these customs were observed, the Battalion officers arranged their work to conform, and although no great progress was evident on any one line the programme as a whole went steadily forward. On the 6th the working parties of the 16th Rifle Brigade were withdrawn from that until the following midnight, in view of the expected enemy retaliation on Ypres, when the British barrage opened. At 8.30 p.m. on the 6th a night party of 15 other ranks of "A" Company under Capt. Anderson, was met in St. Jean by a working party of 75 other ranks of the 16th Rifle Brigade, it being intended to place two working parties on the St. Jean-Potijze road. It was impossible, however, to start then as the British 6-inch batteries nearby were being heavily shelled, but when the shelling ceased at 9.30 p.m., an attempt was made to start work. Before the party had laid down their equipment and taken up their tools heavy shelling recommenced, this time setting fire to a farm building nearby containing ammunition, the flames illuminating the area so that work was impossible, as it exposed the working parties to machine gun fire from the enemy positions overlooking the area.

In another spot, however, 200 feet of grading, 400 of fill and a 20-foot culvert were completed by 2 a.m. At 3.12 a.m. the working party on their way to camp heard the terrific explosion ushering in the Messines offensive, the ground rocking and heaving for fully five seconds. This was the signal, as it was immediately followed by gunfire from every battery in the area in unison. At once enemy retaliation became general, although more distributed than usual. The St. Jean-Potijze road, from which they had been withdrawn a few minutes before, was beaten by shrapnel and traversed by machine gun fire, followed by a wave of gas, forcing the men to stand to with respirators. By the time this had passed over, dawn broke, greatly increasing the usual vigilance of the enemy for any movement in the sector, making it necessary for the men to break into small parties on returning to camp. During the day the enemy shelled Ypres intensively, particularly from the north. As the Battalion's working parties and all infantry units had been withdrawn from the sector, all work had to be carried out by the unit itself. In fact, save for a few military policemen, the personnel of the Battalion were the only living souls visible in the town. All efforts were concentrated on keeping open lines already built and although the men had to be continually withdrawn from one part of the work to another, no casualties were suffered until 5 p.m., when a shell burst in the centre of a party, killing one and wounding five.

On the lines leading to Ypres hostile shelling was extremely heavy all day, requiring parties to be continually on the alert to repair breaks. In the early morning, shelling of the lines destroyed 15 rail lengths, which were replaced, but not before two casualties occurred. On 8th June instructions came to double track the line to Atherley Junction.

On the 5th in Ypres "A" Company succeeded in laying steel across the Plains d'Amour and on a second line as far as the railway station along the road bridge under construction under great difficulties because of gas and lachramatory shells, forcing the men to wear their respirators frequently. In the night of the 8th/9th, the canal near the dugouts was subjected to a heavy bombardment by gas shells. The men had to stand to wearing respirators from 2 until 3 a.m., which was particularly trying after working hard all day. The next day the work of laying in road crossings to connect all steel laid the previous three days was begun. Three crossings were made, one at Rue d'Elverdinghe, one at Windy Corner and a third at the railway station spur.

Considerable work was entailed in these crossings, as the streets were paved with blocks of stone with a high crown. The work was again increased as the rails of the old civil tramway were still intact. The first two crossings, moreover, were under balloon observation, but the task was completed on the 10th, and also a curved crossing.

On the previous night enemy shelling completely destroyed 200 feet of track and grade laid across the Plains d'Amour, which was not repaired until the following day, when "B" Company relieved "A", patched up the grade, but were prevented from relaying the steel by enemy shell fire. On the 11th, however, the breaks were repaired, and 1,300 feet of track was laid towards St. Jean. The next day all attempts to do any work were prevented, practically all the work done in Ypres being destroyed and lines adjacent to buildings buried under brick. In the afternoon steel laying was started to repair several breaks totalling about 300 feet. After being shelled off several times, the parties were withdrawn, with the loss of one wounded. The parties withdrew to another line, also badly damaged, where again they were driven away, moving to a point between the Canal and the Railway Square to ballast, but a third time were shelled off the job, a brick building collapsing on the track.

In the afternoon, however, the demolished track in the first two lines was repaired and the building near the Canal removed, but as the shelling continued heavily the men were sent to camp to stand by until night fell. In the evening 1,200 feet of track were connected, while a second party went to St. Jean and laid 450 feet of steel, although forced to carry the sections more than 500 feet. Later in the evening both parties were driven off and compelled to take shelter in adjacent dugouts. Lieut. H.B.W. Smith and a party of a Labour Company attempting to grade near the St. Jean-Potijze road came under a heavy bombardment of gas and shrapnel shells, some taking cover in ditches and others scattering. While rounding them up and accounting for them, Lieut. Smith was slightly gassed, and on returning to camp all were forced to keep on their respirators because of the gas bombardment, which had also been laid on the Canal. In crossing the fill in the Canal over which ran one of the light railways, several of the party fell into the water in the dark and wearing respirators, and were rescued with difficulty. Lieut. Smith and two other ranks were slightly gassed and Spr. Boone so seriously he was sent to hospital. On 13th June little progress was again made in Ypres, and another sapper was wounded and another gassed. On the following day the unit was instructed to cease all new work in the town and keep only a strong maintenance party at work repairing any lines over which supplies were urgently required.

Since arriving in this area, the unit had found that much time was wasted through the inexperience of some controls of the operating company, the system on which they worked not being suitable for construction work. Instead of allowing two trains to meet within a block and making full use of passing sidings and spurs, one or other would invariably be held at the control until the other passed. This system led to many aggravating delays with a large number of men whose employment depended on a regular supply of material. As the unit's parties worked in two shifts, and the shelling of all forward areas forced them to live so far back, an attempt was made to arrange a time table of work trains to take them to the scene of their labour, but this did not succeed, as trains failed to appear at the time specified, so the men walked and the unit lost much of their effectiveness. Work started on the double track to White Pole Corner with sectional steel, but apart from that work west of Ypres was confined to building spurs and sidings and the patrol of all lines with strong maintenance parties to assure ammunition and supplies reaching their destination.

In the early spring the unit's Ladies' Auxiliary in Canada sent a supply of garden seed at the suggestion of Col. Clarke. These were planted at Velu by permission of the Vth Army. Implements were secured by the simple method of picking up those left lying in the fields and volunteers were never lacking to assist in the work of cultivation in their spare time. Planting was done in several stages with the result that from June until the end of September a continuous supply of fresh vegetables sufficient for the whole unit was issued. Not only was it a luxury, but it contributed to maintain the good health of the men.

On investigating a large number of damaged machine shops after the German retreat, Lieut. Ternan found some which, with very little work, could be used, so he collected these, repaired and set them up in a broad gauge car, and with the tools in the regular equipment made a shop capable of turning out almost any type of work, and proved very valuable in making repairs.

On 1st July a training camp opened at Watou with half of "A" Company, and on the 3rd the 12th Battalion,

King's Own Yorkshire Light Infantry Pioneers, arrived. As a result of the experience gained at this training camp, it was decided that the work in the advanced area should be carried on in two shifts, one starting at daylight and continuing until noon, and the second beginning at noon and finishing at dark. In August, for example, that shift started at four and finished at 8 p.m. It was arranged that the surveys should follow as closely as possible the projected line shown on the map, which was laid down to conform to the contour of the ground, and the main points the Army wished to reach. The starting point of the work was at the Ypres Canal.

The plan called for a reconnaissance party of one officer and three other ranks going ahead as soon as daylight permitted, to picket out a line, using tall pickets with red flags at frequent intervals to guide the locating party following. They would take note of the requirements at each water course, road, deep trench or other obstruction where special material would be required, as shown on the projected line on their maps. All reports were to be made on special forms and sent to Advance Headquarters, Canadian Railway Troops, where a material yard would be prepared containing a supply of rails, sleepers, culvert pipe, bridge material and rail sections, to enable special cars of material to be loaded and despatched to arrive in proper series at the places at which they were required.

The reconnaissance party would be followed by a location party of one instrument man and six other ranks, assisted by the tall pickets with red flags placed by the reconnaissance party, staking out the lines, the stakes to be placed every 100 feet on the tangent and marked with the number of the station on the side facing the rear, with a hub driven at the back of each stake, flush with the ground. When 2,500 feet of the centre line was completed, a report was to be sent to Advance Headquarters giving the alignment notes to enable the officer in charge of the material yard to make up the material train with the right amount of straight and curved sections, it being unnecessary to have the material loaded on the train in the order in which it would be laid. There would, however, be a sufficient number of waggons of curved sections in that particular part of the line. The location party would be followed by a levelling party of one instrument man, one rodman and two other ranks taking levels on the hubs at each station stake along the location line, and as many intermediate points as were necessary to obtain the true surveys of the ground between stations. One turning point in every 1,500 feet would be referenced and used as a bench mark. When 1,500 feet of levels were completed, the instrument man would reduce his notes and plot a profile of his line, giving the approximate chainage of his construction, and placing a grade line not exceeding one in 100 against traffic and 1.5 in 100 with traffic. He would then compute his cuts and fills for each station; list them, and send it to the officer in charge of grading before proceeding with the next 1,500 feet of line.

The grading parties were now ready to begin work. The officer in charge of grading would have told off his 12 grading parties and given the sapper in charge the amount of cut or fill at the stations between which he would be working. This cut or fill would be marked in chalk on the back of the station stake and signify that the distance should be graded below or above the grade plug, which was driven flush with the ground by the locating party. As each grading party finished the task allotted, they would move forward in charge of their sappers to the next station on the line. The grading would thus move forward 1,200 feet to a task. As soon as the first 100 feet of grading was completed the track laying would begin, following the grading party closely. The culvert and bridge parties would also move forward to the place where the first culvert or bridge was to be inserted to prepare the drain for laying the pipe or make excavations in the side of the bank for placing the mud sills and bridge bents. When all preparations were made, they would return to the train, offload and carry forward the material for the culvert or bridge, and exert every effort to have it ready so as not to delay the track laying. Immediately following the track laying party was the rough lining and ballast party, lining the track behind the steel train and levelling irregularities in the formation by filling in with earth. The sand ballast trains would then be brought up, and the offloading and lifting party would place the sand under the sleepers. The number of troops and their classification was computed and tabulated for each of the above duties.

At a conference in the office of the Assistant Director of Light Railways on 29th June to discuss organizing the light railways in the IInd and Vth Army areas, arrangements were made for organizing a training ground for Light Railway Troops, each Light Railway Battalion to be allotted two Pioneer Battalions in addition to the two Labour Companies already attached. The plan for the summer operations in the Ypres Salient required four lines of light railway to be pushed forward: one for the Fourteenth Corps, adjoining the French on the north; a second for the Eighteenth Corps adjoining the Fourteenth Corps on the north and the Nineteenth Corps in front of Ypres; a third for the Nineteenth Corps in front of Ypres as far south as the Ypres-Zonnebeeke standard gauge railway, and a fourth for the Second Corps just south of the Ypres-Zonnebeeke railway.

The third line was allotted to Col. Clarke for construction by the 2nd Battalion, Canadian Railway Troops, and its two attached Pioneer Battalions, assisted by the two Labour Companies, which were to look after the forwarding of material and the maintenance of the lines in rear. After the opening of the training depot at Watou on 1st July with the arrival of half "A" Company, the arrival of the 12th Battalion, King's Own Yorkshire Light Infantry Pioneers on the 3rd, and the receipt at the camp of railway material and assembling it at Bandagham broad gauge railhead, the officers of the camp were given a lecture on the 7th by the Assistant Director of Light Railways 5, at which Gen. Harrison, Director of Light Railways, and Lieut.-Col. Reynolds, D.G.T., General Headquarters, were present, and the question of methods of construction in the forward area was discussed. It was decided that tests be made over broken ground so that those carrying out the work could be quickly divided. The first test was made by the 2nd Canadian Railway Troops on the afternoon of the 13th.

Twelve grade parties consisting of 25 Pioneers each were in charge of one Engineer Officer and five Pioneer Officers, with 12 Sappers to assist. They began work at 12.30 p.m.

on a line previously surveyed by the 2nd Canadian Railway Troops survey party, followed almost immediately by a bridge and culvert party of six 2nd Canadian Railway Troops and 25 Pioneers. At 1 p.m. the track laying party began work on the new formation completed by the grading party. They consisted of four platelayers of the 2nd C.R.T. and 10 Pioneers. A rough lining and earth packing party of one Sapper, 2nd C.R.T., and 12 Pioneers followed, and then a carrying party of 70 Pioneers, 64 of whom carried rail sections from the train with rail tongs specially made by the 2nd C.R.T. for the purpose, and placed them on the formation, and six assisting the platelayers to connect. One section of rail was carried by eight men with four sets of tongs so that the men walked on each side of the formation and carried the section well over the heads of the platelayers. In this manner the steel was placed in front of the track laying party without interfering in their work. The train crew consisted of two engineers, one guard, 2nd C.R.T., and 2 Sappers, 2nd C.R.T., in charge of offloading material, with a Pioneer Officer in charge of the party.

The rail sections were loaded on the waggons side by side and ten sections high, so that 335 feet of track complete was carried on each waggon. The train consisted of four waggons of steel, one of which might be curved sections and one of culvert and bridging material, so each train contained one-quarter mile of track material. The test was carried out until 4 p.m., during which time the school was visited by a number of light railway staff officers and others interested in railway work. In the three and a half hours, 1,200 feet of steel was laid and 2,600 feet of formation completed, two 14-foot bridges had been built which the steel train passed over and six box culverts were put in place.

The second test on the 15th started at 12 noon and finished at 5 p.m., in which interval 2,600 feet was graded and 1,400 feet of track laid, one bridge was built and six culverts were placed. Heavier cuts and fills this time made the work more difficult, about 400 feet of the work being in a cutting from two to $2\frac{1}{2}$ feet deep. A final test took place on the 17th of the first class, beginning at 1 p.m., the formation being far enough ahead for the tracklaying party to start at 1.45. By 6 p.m., 3,300 feet of formation had been completed and 2,800 feet of track laid, two 14-foot bridges and one 40-foot bridge built, which the steel train traversed; eight box culverts had been put in the formation and one road crossing was built. The actual time of working on the formation was four hours, 22 minutes, and on tracklaying three hours, 13 minutes. The work was stopped at different stages to give special instructions how it should be carried on under service conditions. The finished results were, therefore, 100 feet of track laid in every seven minutes of working time, or 6,972 feet in eight hours.

It was felt that the schooling was of benefit to the 2nd C.R.T. as well as to the Pioneer units they were training, as it enabled the men to experiment with various methods of tracklaying. It was found that by carrying the track over cars and off the end of the train and over the heads of the platelayers time was saved. To do that, long-handled tongs had to be made and by using four sets of these to each rail section, eight men could handle a section conveniently. Again, drift pins were used by the forward platelayers to enable them to connect the sections with speed, these pins being removed by the platelayers behind the tracklaying party and the fish-plate bolts put in and tightened before the train passed. By keeping the train 200 to 300 feet from the tracklayers, a small lining party and rough ballasting party could do their work before the train moved forward. After each test, the officers held a conference with the non-commissioned officers and senior men of the 2nd C.R.T. and King's Own Yorkshire Light Infantry at which the work of the previous day was discussed and suggestions were made by both officers and other ranks on improvements. Many useful ideas were thus tried and if successful embodied in the training.

On the 18th the troops attending the first school returned to the forward area about Ypres, and a second class organized from half "B" Company, 2nd C.R.T., a company of the 9th Gordon Highlanders Pioneers, a company of the 16th Royal Irish Rifles Pioneers, a company of the 11th Hants and a company of the 1st/4th South Lancashire

Pioneers. The next day a lecture was given all officers, non-commissioned officers and senior men of "B" Company, 2nd C.R.T., and the Pioneer attached units; the proposed scheme of the advance was outlined, and the method of training was explained in detail so that a test on construction might be carried out the following day, when the first test was made, the parties arranged similarly to those in the first school. On the 23rd a special test was made for the officers of the Nineteenth Corps Headquarters, the feature of the day's work being the building of a 40-foot bridge over a dry creek on the training ground. The bridge was carried forward on a special car attached to the steel train, and when the track arrived within 100 yards of the location where the bridge was to be built, the bridge culvert party offloaded the material, six 9-inch steel girders, two 5-foot framed bridge bents, timber for mud sills and bracing and bridge sleepers. The material was carried forward to the site and in 17 minutes from the time the train stopped, the bridge was complete; the track laid across it, and the steel train passed over it. In the day's test, 3,800 feet of formation was made complete and 3,500 feet of track laid, with a 14-foot bridge and a 40-foot bridge in four hours. On 25th July, in a final test of the second school of four hours, steel was laid at a rate of 1,050 feet an hour, and the formation was kept well in advance of the steel. The limits of the camp did not allow the line being extended farther.

If the formation were difficult to construct, the number of grading parties could be increased, but it was found inadvisable to employ more than 25 on 100 feet of formation. Special parties from the Labour Companies could be employed in loading and offloading the ballast and railway material trains, 600 men being available for this purpose. To carry on the work continuously, it was found necessary to have eight trains available for track material, for each shift, which would require four tractors and 40 waggons. The material would be taken forward from the steel dump by locomotives and placed in forward loops, where it could be taken on by the tractors, four trains moving up with the morning and four with the afternoon shift. The ballast trains would be worked similarly with four trackers and 128 waggons. This sand would be forwarded by locomotives from the sand dump, eight waggons to a train and eight trains to a shift, thus giving 64 waggons of sand to every mile of track. This sand would be taken forward in convoys of four trains of four waggons each, thus each tractor would have to make four trips to the forward area to get the 64 waggons forward in each shift. The equipment needed, therefore, in the forward area for building two miles a day was eight tractors, 40 flat waggons and 128 box waggons.

CHAPTER V

THE YPRES OFFENSIVE

The division between the Messines and the Ypres offensives of 1917 is difficult to place with precision, because the preparation for the latter may be said to have begun immediately after the enemy retaliation following the former had died away. On 18th June, a heavy bombardment in the sector west of the town smashed 500 feet of track on the line to White Pole Corner near the latter spot, and 675 feet on another line, but both were repaired that day. The following day the bombardment continued, many breaks occurring and two more brick buildings collapsing on one of the lines. The maintenance party living in the dugouts on the Canal and working in the town on returning for lunch found the 4.5 howitzer battery opposite their camp under a heavy bombardment and were unable to approach until 3 p.m. At 5.30 p.m. this bombardment was resumed, several direct hits occurring on the dugouts, but their construction withstood it. One shell, however, struck the tool store and scattered it over a wide radius, destroying many tools. A report from the Operating Company on the 21st that a line then carrying heavy traffic had been broken by shell fire after maintenance parties working along it that day had reported all clear to the batteries, caused Capt. Anderson to make a personal inspection. Walking the entire length, he found that a shell had destroyed the last section at the extreme end of the line.

At the request of the Assistant Director of Light Railways, "B" Company began work on the 23rd on one of the central lines, but owing to severe shelling little could be accomplished. Several men were knocked down and buried, but no serious results accrued. Lieut. Graham inspected another line turned over to the unit and found that 2,300 feet of tracklaying, ditching and bolting was required. At 4 p.m. Lieut. Jenkins and a party laid 1,900 feet of this line, Lieut. Smith with a tractor keeping him supplied with material. The work here was within the Belgian line, and, in fact, in front of their reserve trenches, so was easy to do, as that part of the country was free from shellfire. By the next day the laying of steel on both the former lines referred to was completed. On the 29th a shell made a direct hit on Barrie Ammunition Dump, which was almost destroyed by several explosions, and when the fire died down, Capt. Anderson inspected it, finding that 150 feet had been destroyed. As this was a double track spur, ammunition trains could operate until the break was repaired. Col. Clarke attended a conference at the Headquarters of the Assistant Director of Light Railways that day to discuss future operations and the formation of the training school described previously, and also to co-ordinate the work of his men and that of the Pioneer Battalions to be attached to his unit.

Because of the need of having a definite supply of water for engines in the Vth Army area, Lieut. Ternan was loaned to the Assistant Director of Light Railways to take charge of the water supply in that area. On investigation, he advised the erection of seven tanks on two of the systems varying from 1,000 to 5,000 gallons, so a party was detailed permanently from one of the attached Labour units for this project. The constant source of trouble in construction was found in the switches, which appeared to have been turned out in the shops without being fitted or tested in any way. When laid on the ground they failed to line properly and their turnout was of such close gauge that a tractor or locomotive with a wheel base in any way stiff would derail unless driven very slowly. In preparation for the advance, an experienced man was detailed to overhaul and fit the parts together, marking each he passed as ready for use. The centre separating block of each guard rail was removed in each case and the bolt tightened, drawing the ball of the guard rail to within 1½ inches of the ball of the running rail, which was in the main sufficient to prevent derailment. Another source of difficulty, beyond remedy in the field, was in the frogpoint, the majority of switches supplied the unit for the advance being made with a split point instead of the solid point. This point would not withstand traffic for more than a week, but would gradually open and lose its shape, causing derailments, so these were reserved as far as possible for little used sidings and the solid points for the main line.

Col. Walter Hill Moodie (1), 9th Battalion, Canadian Railway Troops, visited the unit to arrange to take over part of its system for maintenance, to give the Battalion a free hand in its preparation for the advance. It was agreed that his unit take over all lines except that to White Pole Corner from a point known as the Triangle to White Pole Corner and the central line from White Pole Corner to the village of St. Jean. As the main line of the 2nd Battalion's advance, the unit retained the line mentioned so as to make what arrangements they wished for storage of material previous to zero hour. On 8th July a location was made for a forward dump for storage of steel and other railway material. A party of 100 had for some time been assembling steel at the triangle and the construction of this spur was required to enable the unit to relieve the congestion at the assembling point. This dump was chosen east of Machine Gun Farm road in an open plain, which although affording no cover from observation, was well away from any well-defined ranging point. In the early part of the month a spur had been built parallel to the broad gauge, where it was proposed to establish a sand dump. One train daily had been arriving for some time, until by the end of the month some 1,000 broad gauge trucks had been piled in a huge dump.

Although officially, the work of the Battalion from zero hour was begun at the Canal in the dull period in July, as much as possible had been done in ballasting and preparing the grade as far as St. Jean. Forward of that point Lieut. Graham and a survey party of "B" Company on a day of comparative quiet continued the location along the main line, a distance of 2,400 feet to Pagoda Wood as far as the reserve trenches. Early on 12th July the enemy shelled the Battalion transport, killing two and wounding Lieut. L.F. Johnston, the transport officer. In response to a request from the Battalion on the 20th, Lieut. R.E. Spalding was detailed to the unit in charge of operating in the forward area in the advance. The next day location was made for a locomotive yard on ground selected by the South African Operating Company, who had been detailed to operate

---

(1) D.S.O.

the 2nd Battalion's lines in the advance. This yard chosen was known as "Culloden". That evening the ammunition dump at Orillia siding was blown, demolishing 450 feet of track and grade.

In heavy shelling of the main line crossing the Yser Canal on the 26th, a shell made a direct hit, setting fire to two trucks of ammunition, and almost simultaneously another shell burst on the track a few feet in front of the locomotive, the boiler and forepart of the latter being riddled with splinters. Before the train could be stopped, the locomotive dropped into the shell hole, toppling over on its side and blocking the line. This was cleared by 1 p.m. the next day. On the evening of the 28th Battalion Headquarters moved to a rendezvous where all Pioneers and Labour units had bivouaced that day. At 2.30 a.m. on the 31st, "A" Company and attached Pioneers stood by at the advanced Headquarters until 4.15 before going forward to start construction. At 3.50 a.m. the barrage opened, beginning far to the north and spreading until the whole front was flaming. The unit's first task was to fill shell holes between the Canal and St. Jean and repair breaks in the steel already laid. In moving forward, the men were fortunately well strung out, for in crossing the Yser Canal a shell struck the side of the embankment, wounding four. The morning was foggy with a drizzling rain rendering observation impossible, but enemy shelling was active, principally shrapnel. In the morning steel was laid on the main line and in the afternoon grading was done on the Wieltje Spur. Rain came after the drizzle and continued all day in a steady downpour, which, while unpleasant, made it possible to continue with the work unmolested. On 1st August regular shifts began, "A" Company and attached Pioneers taking the first from 4 a.m. until noon and then "B" and attached Pioneers from that time until 8 p.m. On the Wieltje Spur 1,500 feet were graded and on the Potijze Spur 1,400 feet, while 900 feet of ballasting were done on the main line. The newly laid track quickly disappeared in the mud, but the sand saved the situation, forming a mat and keeping the track from sinking. Continuous maintenance was necessary on all lines because of shell fire.

The programme was somewhat altered by the tactical situation on 2nd August, all efforts being made to grade and complete the line through Ypres to St. Jean and Potijze. In the morning steel was laid from the former to the latter place and in the afternoon through Ypres. During the day 3,500 feet was graded and 2,400 feet of steel laid. Steel was also laid on the main line, which was ballasted, and surveys were pushed forward on it. Casualties the previous day were two killed and one wounded of the attached Pioneers and on this day one of the 2nd C.R.T. wounded and two of the Pioneers wounded. The following day 2,000 feet of grading was completed, 2,000 feet of steel laid and 2,000 feet of ballasting was done on the line running to St. Jean. That day most of the line had to be relifted because of the heavy rains. As much as one truck of sand to two track lengths was sometimes required. The next day on this line 1,000 feet was graded and 2,000 feet of steel laid, and on the Wieltje Spur 800 feet was graded. The stream crossing this line between Ypres and Potijze was spanned by a bridge 73 feet long. Previously built standard bents in the stock in the yard were used, so the structure was completed in an hour. Throughout the day shelling was general, causing many breaks and one man of the 2nd C.R.T. was wounded.

Steel laying on the same line on the 5th was completed, 2,600 feet being laid, while ballast was kept close to the steel, 5,000 feet being laid. In the morning grading and laying steel was carried on a cross line from Labrique to Burnt Farm to connect with the Eighteenth Corps mail line, called for to feed the batteries in the Burnt Farm group. A total of 3,100 feet of track laying was done, and in the evening to accommodate ammunition during the night, 200 feet of steel was laid on the Wieltje Spur and 200 on the main line by a small special party. Some 2,800 feet of grading was completed the following day on the Burnt Farm line and 1,800 feet of steel laid. Several sidings and spurs were also graded and laid on the line to St. Jean and efforts were made to consolidate that already laid. That day two men of the 2nd C.R.T. were wounded.

The 147th Battery applied to have five 60-pounder guns moved to Outskirt Farm, as it was impossible to move them by road since the latter were impassable from the rain, so Lieut. Ternan took charge of the loading and offloading, the first gun being loaded in an hour and placed in its new position at 2 p.m. The second was loaded in 14 minutes after the proper procedure was studied. The remaining guns were moved up the next day. On the 8th the 351st Siege Battery asked to have one of their guns, damaged by shell fire, moved to a point as near the Ordnance workshop in Poperinghe as possible, so this also was done. During the next few days, work consisted in the continuation of maintenance on all lines and the completion of the Burnt Farm line. Some difficulty was experienced as a result of the tanks crossing the line on soft ground at unprepared points. This difficulty was overcome by taking the matter up with Corps, who ordered that in future the Tanks notify the Battalion of their intended crossing, and also carry a supply of broad gauge sleepers to prevent damage to railway lines. While relaying the central line in Ypres on the 11th, a line almost totally destroyed by shell fire, Capt. H.C. Anderson was struck by a shell fragment, dying in the ambulance station within a few minutes. Second in command of "A" Company, he had been promoted since his arrival in France for his efficiency and his death was a loss to the Battalion. The next day work started on the production of a line to join the line to the village of St. Jean and on a cross line to connect with the IInd Army system near the Ypres Asylum.

After a night of heavy artillery preparation, at 4.40 a.m. on the 16th an intense barrage started. Construction was resumed at 5.30 a.m. and that morning 500 feet were graded on the main line east of St. Jean and on the Wieltje Spur 1,500 feet. On the main line 2,000 feet of steel was laid and 1,400 feet of ballast. The survey party completed the location of the Wieltje Spur to Lythance. That morning two of the attached Pioneers were wounded. Major Elliott reported the courageous action of Spr. L. Fenwick of "A" Company, who was with the grading party on the Wieltje Spur. When an enemy shell alighted near the grade, wounding an officer and an other rank of the Royal Engineers Signals working nearby, Spr. Fenwick rushed to assist, and while picking the man up a second shell burst near him. Fortunately he escaped injury; fell flat at once, and without hesitation continued his efforts and helped carry the wounded out of immediate danger. On a previous occasion, he showed similar promptness and courage when Spr. Bowron was wounded at Triangle Camp. For his plucky act he was awarded the Military Medal.

In the afternoon "B" Company on the Wieltje Spur completed 700 feet of grading, 2,500 feet of steel and 900 of ballasting. The survey party located the spur along Cambridge road, a distance of 4,100 feet and the main line 3,300 feet. On the morning of the 17th, "A" Company completed grading the Wieltje Spur and 1,000 feet on the main line. Steel laying was interrupted that morning by enemy shelling. In the afternoon 1,300 feet of steel was laid on the main line and grading was continued for 650 feet. In the next few days a small amount of construction was done, the remainder of the work being maintenance. On the 19th in an air raid a bomb destroyed the dugout occupied by Lieut. Smith at the Sand Dump, burying him and wounding two other ranks. At 4.45 a.m. on the 22nd a barrage opened on the Nineteenth Corps front and construction work was resumed. In the morning 1,000 feet was graded east of Oxford on the main line, 2,060 feet of steel was laid on the spur parallel to the Cambridge road and ballasting followed close on the steel. In the afternoon 900 feet of steel was laid on the Cambridge Road Spur. One member of the survey party was wounded in the eye by a shell splinter. That day about 500 wounded were brought from Wieltje Dressing Station and Cambridge Road Dressing Station to Atherley Junction. Large quantities of gas used by the enemy during the night still pervaded the area and although not strong enough to do real harm, it caused some sickness among the men.

General maintenance was carried on until 27th August, when an attack was made that afternoon. No construction was attempted as the lines were then well forward with the guns, but strong maintenance patrols kept the lines open for the evacuation of the wounded. The attack went in at 3 p.m. in a heavy rain which began an hour earlier, allowing few cases to come in that night. After obtaining authority to use it, brick in large quantities was hauled from Ypres and used as ballast on all lines in the next few days. On 1st September "A" and "B" Companies were relieved by the other two, who returned from Bergues and continued maintenance and consolidation of lines. "C" Company built the Pottenhoek Railhead and "D" an ammunition spur to a 9-inch howitzer battery near Potijze.

In September Lieut. Ternan at the machine shop built a hand lorry from salvage material for use on the track. The frame consisted of the lower part of a damaged tip truck, the drive wheels from the discarded frames of the wheels of a Ford car and the gearing from the damaged material in a lace factory in Ypres. The car was fitted with a brake and clutch, and two men could with ease travel at eight miles an hour. The lorry proved of great help to maintenance patrols in carrying tools and moving about the lines. On 27th September, "C" and "D" Companies were in turn relieved by "A" and "B". The next day a heavy bombardment was put down in the vicinity of St. Jean. At 2.30 p.m. Major Elliott and Lieut. McIlwraith with a party of "A" Company went forward to repair breaks in the main line. Major Elliott was struck by a shell splinter, which killed him instantly. He was buried the following day in Poperinghe Military Cemetery, his funeral being attended by "A" Company and officers from all attached units, with whom he had been popular. Says the diarist, "His death was a severe blow to his Company, who loved him to a man for his kindly and fatherly manner."

Brig.-Gen. J.W. Stewart (2) and Lt.-Col. the Hon. A. MacDonell (3) visited Battalion Headquarters on 6th August to notify Col. Clarke that "C" and "D" Companies would move from the Coxyde area to do maintenance for a short time at Bergues, so the work at the coast was turned over to the 10th Battalion, Canadian Railway Troops, the next day, and "C" and "D" entrained for Bergues, de-

---

(2) Later Major-General. C.B., *London Gazette*, 1.1.19; C.M.G., L.G., 4.6.17; four times mentioned in despatches.

(3) Later Colonel. C.B., *London Gazette*, 3.6.19; C.M.G., L.G., 3.6.18; twice mentioned in despatches and name brought to notice of Secretary of State for War.

training the next day and then pitching camp. "C" Company was allotted about 4,500 feet of double track to be lifted, ballasted and surfaced on the main line from Dunkerque to Proven. Part of it was very wet and spongy, the drainage needing improvement. A survey party marked off the company's section of the work and subdivided it for the working parties. The next day 125 other ranks of "D" Company and 150 attached Labour began work on their part of the line, clearing the sand and mud from between the rails and making ready for lifting more than 2,200 feet of track. "C" Company's section was from Bergues Exchange eastward 1,400 yards. On the 11th, Capt. Craig certified to the Railway Traffic Officer that that night all lines under maintenance could be operated with safety, but that reasonable care should be taken east of Bergues Exchange. While the work continued from day to day, the problem of drainage received special attention. On the 29th the two companies entrained for Proven and thence marched to the Battalion Rest Camp at Watou, and then relieved "A" and "B" Companies as recorded.

Lt.-Gen. H. Watts, Commanding Nineteenth Corps, brought to the notice of the Army Commander "the excellent work done" by all ranks of the 2nd C.R.T. in the operations of 31st July and subsequently, in maintaining the lines and building new ones through Ypres to Potijze, St. Jean and Wieltje, "under most difficult circumstances of weather, ground and shell fire." Maj.-Gen. M.M. Sargent, Deputy Adjutant and Quartermaster General, Vth Army, forwarded the thanks of the Army Commander, who "considers that Lieut.-Col. Clarke and 2nd Battalion, Canadian Railway Troops, deserve great credit for what they have done.... It is realized that most of the work had to be carried out under very difficult conditions, and the results achieved speak very well for the spirit and morale displayed by all concerned." The Assistant Director of Light Railways, IVth Army, Brig.-Gen. J.H. Harrison, endorsed these sentiments.

CHAPTER VI

ADVANCE CAMP, STEEL DUMP

On arrival in the Ypres area again, "D" Company at once was set to repairing breaks in the line at White Pole Corner, Artillery Junction and on the Bedlington Line 1st September, while both companies, parties of the 12th King's Own Yorkshire Light Infantry Pioneers and a company of the 1st/5th Duke of Cornwall's Light Infantry continued maintenance on the system east of the Canal. On the Bedlington line near St. Jean breaks were repaired, necessitating the replacement of 14 sections of steel. Spr. J.S. Cappus was wounded in several places by shell fragments. Half "B" Company continued with maintenance with 290 of the 141st Labour Company on the lines between Woestenhoek and Culloden the following day, resurfacing, and a 35-foot siding was built. Two Companies of the 12th K.O.Y.L.I. Pioneers, one company of the 1st/4th South Lancashires and the 192nd Labour Company were attached to "C" Company as labour, to proceed with the construction and maintenance of the lines from Culloden east to the Yser Canal, and work began on Mission Junction Terminal. A party of "D" Company and 100 of the 12th K.O.Y.L.I., grading on the gun spur from Potijze at the end of the Morpeth line, had to stop for four hours because of shell fire, but during this period they were employed in ballasting on the spur to St. Jean. Parties under Lieut. Sharp working on a 15-inch howitzer gun spur, completed it under shell fire.

On the Mission Junction Terminal, 2,650 feet of steel was laid the next day, and 300 at the Stanley Salvage Dump, where three turnouts were installed and 600 feet was graded to the last joint. That day the unit received 918 Lee Enfield rifles complete. Parties working on the 9-inch howitzer gun spur under Lieut. Galbraith were shelled on the 4th, making it necessary to withdraw three times. Spr. R. Chapman of "D" Company was killed by a direct hit by a 5.9-inch shell, while working near Gibraltar Farm. The same shell also killed one Sergeant and one Private, and wounded three other privates of the 12th K.O.Y.L.I. Pioneers, one of the wounded dying *en route* to the dressing station. In the afternoon Spr. Chapman was buried in the Poperinghe Military Cemetery, Hon. Capt. H.J. Allan officiating. The following evening the vicinity of "B" Company's camp was bombed by enemy aircraft. That night it was necessary for the troops in the Advance Camp and the Steel Dump to wear gas respirators for a short time because of enemy mustard gas shells. Because of enemy shell fire in the forward areas the following morning, it was decided to work in two shifts. With his working parties that day, Lieut. Knox had to withdraw from the 9-inch howitzer spur at the end of the Morpeth line on account of heavy rifle fire, so he had to proceed with ballasting on the Bedlington line. Six breakages were repaired on that line, two holes were filled, and steel was replaced where the line had been blown by aerial bombs.

In the early morning of the 6th, a shell alighted in "B" Company's camp, but did no damage. Sgt. J.A. Joyce with two other ranks of the South African Railway Operating Company, put out a fire caused by an enemy bomb dropping in the 2nd/1st North Midland Artillery Dump at great personal risk. [1] During the night too a number of bombs had dropped near the Advance Camp, and one exploded in the camp area that day, but there were no casualties. On one of the loops six blowouts caused by large calibre shells were repaired, and a broken section of the Forest Hall line was replaced. Lieut. Ternan completed the installation of a water system the following day at Vox Vris Yard, the work including the erection of a 5,000 gallon cast iron tank on a 15-foot trestle; the laying of 4-inch pipe with valves and fittings, and the erection of four standpipes at various points in the yard. Two platoons of "B" Company under Capt. Adams attended a dedicating service of crosses to be erected in Poperinghe Military Cemetery on the 9th on the graves of Cpl. Learmouth and Spr. Walsh, the Chaplain officiating. One of the 92nd Labour Company was wounded by shrapnel that day.

---

(1) Sgt. Joyce was awarded the Military Medal, *London Gazette*, 19th November, 1917.

That night enemy shell fire was observed near the Triangle (2), and as a result four sections of steel had to be replaced there. That day the work in Ypres was hampered by enemy shrapnel. Lieut. Ternan and a party completed the erection of a 1,000-gallon tank at Culloden, and 500 feet of 2-inch pipe was laid from the pump-house at the Canal to the tank for filling. Valves and a connection for washing out boilers were placed in the pipe line. That day also the workshop completed making new grates and fire-boxes for Headquarters and "B" Company field kitchens. In the evening "B" Company held a series of boxing bouts, members of the Bermudan Garrison Artillery attending. Rifle exercises started on the 11th, "A" Company spending half an hour on those and an hour in physical training. Grading, steel laying, ballasting and lining and the placing of a second road crossing on the Ypres ballast spur completed this task, but for two and a quarter hours the work was discontinued because of the severity of enemy shelling. A party under Lieut. Sharp of "D" Company had to stop work in the afternoon for the same reason. The next night a heavy enemy bombardment caused many breaks in the forward section of the lines, four of them being repaired by the night party of "D" Company. The next morning the chief task was in repairing the night's breaks.

At Watou Camp on the 13th Col. Clarke with Major Gibson inspected "A" Company, who then continued company and platoon drill. "C" Company completed Pottenhoek (3) Railhead, except for rebuilding a bridge, which was begun. On the Asylum Spur, Ypres, 600 feet of old

---

(2) The 2nd C.R.T. Forward Camp and Canadian Dump were just west of White Pole Junction north-west of Ypres; Atherley Junction west of them and just northeast of Vlamertinghe; Culloden Locomotive Yard to the northwest of Atherley; the Triangle west of Culloden, and Woestenhoek Yard to the west, lying northeast of Poperinghe.

(3) Mission Junction lay slightly northwest of Atherley Junction and Pottenhoek Spur adjoined the former in a northwesterly direction, almost due north of Vlamertinghe.

track was salvaged and that distance graded and steel was laid. One road crossing was placed and conspicuous portions of the line camouflaged. In the past fortnight, about 75 breaks from shell fire had been repaired. A party of 33 reinforcements from the Canadian Railway Troops Depot, Purfleet, Hants, arrived at Woestenhoek Yard Headquarters Camp the next day, and were distributed among the companies. The ratio of trained railwaymen was small in comparison with other trades. "A" Company left Watou for the Triangle Camp to take over the lines from Woestenhoek Yard to Culloden Sand Dump from "B" Company for the ensuing two weeks, while "B" moved to Watou Camp by motor lorry. Starting that day a Company worked east of the Yser Canal for a fortnight, going to work by train. As the work was more or less under enemy observation, the parties worked in two shifts.

Major Elliott and Lieut. McIlwraith began construction of an ammunition dump siding on the 15th, grading 1,200 feet and laying 900 feet of steel. The spur was ready to receive ammunition by 5 p.m. The line had been located by Lieut. Draper and six other ranks of "A" Company that morning, and the next day 800 feet of Oakhanger Spur, in which Major Elliott and "A" Company laid 400 feet of steel, placed two switches and two 18-foot culverts. In addition, 1,000 feet on this spur was ballasted. At Watou Camp, the Roman Catholics paraded to Houtkerque for Divine Service, and the remainder of the Company attended a church service conducted by Hon. Capt. Allan. In the afternoon the 2nd C.R.T. defeated the 1st C.R.T. at baseball at International Corner. Capt. H.R.H. the Prince of Wales honoured the camp with a visit. The Pickering Loop on the Mannors-Forest Hall Line northeast of Ypres was completed the next day. Three turnouts were repaired at Pickering and Mannors Junction. On the Forest Hall Line, 60 feet of sand put on the track by animal traffic was cleared, 300 feet of steel on Morpeth (south of Mannors Junction) was removed, as it had been damaged by vehicular traffic, and on Forest Hall five shell holes were filled and steel was repaired. Part of the damage was caused by bombs dropped by a squadron of 16 enemy aircraft. "B" Company defeated the American medical men at the 2nd Canadian Casualty Clearing Station the following afternoon. That day six breaks from shell fire were repaired by the use of nine sections of steel, chiefly in the vicinity of St. Jean and east of it.

On the Bedlington Line [4] on the 18th, two shell holes were filled and the steel was replaced, and on the Rotherbury Line (4) six breaks from shell fire were repaired. At 7 p.m., the camps of "D" Company and the 12th K.O.Y.L.I. were shelled, and Spr. R. Turner was seriously wounded, dying on his way to hospital. The latter unit had one killed and two seriously wounded. Two other ranks of the 2nd C.R.T. were sent to Watou Camp, suffering from slight shock. On the Forest Hall Line the following day, two shell holes were filled and the track repaired there and elsewhere in the locality. On the loop at St. Jean, a petrol electric tractor was derailed, toppling over into a shell hole, but the track was repaired here. On the Bedlington Line the next day, owing to the damage by shell fire, it was necessary to rebuild the track for 150 feet. In spite of the fact that the lines were surrounded by large numbers of field guns, little enemy shell fire was noticed in this area. That day Sprs. J. Edwards, J. Leah, S.T. Hayward, W.A. Stovell, W.J. Lewins, J.L. Davey, H.H. McLeod and G.T. Saunders were buried under a wall hit by an enemy shell. They were sent for a week's rest to Watou Camp. Under the supervision of Lieut. Ternan, 1,200 feet of one-inch pipe line was laid in a trench 18 inches deep from the 5,000 gallon tank in Vox Vris Yard to the Vth Army Headquarters Camp.

On the 21st, shell fire near the Advance Camp was heavy. One shell hole was repaired the next day on the Bedlington Line without any delay to traffic and another on the Rotherbury Line. On Forest Hall, the track was broken by shell fire, but was repaired in 45 minutes. At 2.45 p.m. a party repairing grade at St. Jean were shelled off the job, and at Mannors Junction a party was shelled. Sgt. R.B. Rue and Sprs. E.A. Way and Ashton were

---

(4) From Wallsend Junction just above St. Jean to connect with the Rotherbury line parallel to the Cambridge Road.

wounded. Spr. O.L.S. McRae, the only one of the party unhurt, carried Spr. Way to a small tram truck under shell-fire and pushed him several hundred yards to a First Aid Station.

The 2nd Battalion defeated the 1st C.R.T. at the former's camp on the Proven-International Corner Road on the 23rd, among the spectators being Capt. H.R.H. the Prince of Wales, Staff Officers of the Fourteenth Corps and the Assistant Director of Light Railways, Vth Army. Two shell breaks were repaired the next day near St. Jean and three craters and five bent rails repaired on the Rotherbury Line. The following day six sections of steel damaged by shell fire at White Pole Junction were relayed.

On the evening of the 26th, an advance was made by the infantry, necessitating the extension of the forward line. The grading party finding it necessary to repair the old Bedlington Line from Warwick Farm met difficulty on account of the mass of barbed wire and fortifications in the old Hindenburg Line. Two shell breaks on the Bedlington and Forest Hall lines were repaired. Later in the day two more breaks occurred on the latter line, but the heavy shell fire made it impossible to approach the work, but there was no traffic on that line. The night patrol escorted 12 trains of ammunition to points in the forward area. Considerable hostile shell fire was also met the next day, but no casualties occurred. Cpl. J. Aldis and Sprs. J. Harrington and Miller were injured when the steel train passed another train in the siding at Mannors Junction, and as not enough clearance had been allowed, the steel fell off the cars. "A" Company moved to the Advance Camp on the 28th, taking over a number of small splinter-proof dugouts from "D". Major Elliott with parties from "A" Company and 145 K.O.Y.L.I. began work on a new spur, while other parties of "A" with 75 of the 192nd Labour Company did general maintenance on all lines from Culloden forward. In the afternoon, Major Elliott and Lieut. McIlwraith and a party went forward to repair several bad breaks on the Bedlington line.

At St. Jean, severe shelling by the enemy's 9.2s was met, so the party took shelter in the ditch at the side of the road. It was here that Major Elliott was killed almost immediately by a shell fragment, as previously mentioned. Shell fire was severe in all forward positions of the line, on the Bedlington line 250 feet of track being put out of order by three shell holes, which were repaired by 9.45 p.m. The night patrol put in a new switch at Laydon Junction to repair damage done by a derailed engine. In the afternoon, "C" Company left by lorry for Watou Camp for two weeks. The Second Corps (Anzacs) took over from the Fifth Corps at noon that day. On the 29th, Lieut. Ternan completed the manufacture of 35 stoves from oil drums, made in response to Corps orders. More were in preparation and enough were planned to supply the Battalion for the winter. During the month the Headquarters workshop also turned out a "Jim Crow" track bender for narrow gauge rails and a pump car for use on light railways, capable of operation by two men, though it would carry six. It had a maximum speed of 12 miles an hour.

In September more than 175 breaks in the system required the replacement of more than 280 sections of steel. Nearly all were shell breaks occurring east of Ypres. The work of the last day of the month carried the Wilde Wood Spur beyond Zonnebeke road, which made it convenient for the 18-pounder on the spur to draw ammunition from the latter.

The good work of the Canadian Railway Troops in evacuating the wounded in the advance of 20th August was the subject of a letter of appreciation to the Director-General of Transport from the Director-General of Medical Services, Surgeon-General Sir A.T. Sloggett, K.C.B., K.C.M.G., K.C.V.O., who mentioned a feature of much value: the running of small trains taking loads of 60 to 100 at a time, so that the Casualty Clearing Stations were not embarrassed by large numbers of wounded arriving at one time, and were able to deal with them as they came without delay.

Lieut. Ternan, who had been in charge of the repair shop, was detailed to act as second-in-command of "A" Company on 1st October at Woestenhoek Yard, Headquarters Camp. In addition to escorting ammunition trains, the night party of that company rerailed the tractor at Laydon Junction, repairing the track and replacing one section of steel at Woolen Junction. In the morning a bad break on the Bedlington line was repaired using three sections, and a road crossing was put in at Zonnebeke road on the Wilde Wood Line. The afternoon shift of "A" Company could not start work at 1.30 p.m. on account of the shelling. At 4.45 p.m. shell fire again became too heavy to permit any more work. "B" Company had a similar experience on the Forest Hall extension, for the mist clearing at 10.40 a.m., enemy shelling became heavier and work had to cease, but not before Spr. W. Heckbert and Acting Lance Sgt. C. Offerdal were wounded. At 5 p.m. shelling again compelled the parties to leave their work. At Watou Camp Major Craig reorganized "C" Company with platoons and sections as permanent working units, with Lieuts. T.W. Clarke, H.C. Draper, A.R. Clarke and A.O.L. Cameron in command of Nos. 9, 10, 11 and 12 Platoons, respectively. "D" Company was at work with attached labour on the Vlamertinghe Stone Siding, grading, laying steel and ballasting, and inserting a road crossing over the Plank road. One party was on maintenance of the line between Atherley and Culloden resurfacing 1,200 feet, and also from Culloden to the Triangle and from thence to Woestenhoek Yard.

Despite heavy shelling the following morning on the section at the pond at Bill Cottage, "A" Company graded the spur to Wilde Wood and laid 752 feet of steel; filled four water filled shell holes, and put in a culvert to drain the pond. "B" Company and 240 of the 19th Lancashire Fusiliers Pioneers on the Forest Hall extension could do little that day because of the heavy barrage of the British guns from that point. The day was clear and hostile aircraft numerous, parties being heavily shelled off work twice. On the Forest Hall extension the next afternoon, Spr. C.H. Greenbury was killed and Spr. L.S. Mansfield and Spr. P.G. Fraser wounded, and Capt. Gaunt and three other ranks of the King's Own Yorkshire Light Infantry were wounded by the same salvo. The shelling became so heavy that work had to cease at 4.30 p.m.

CHAPTER VII

PASSCHENDAELE

By this time those significant operations of the British offensive known as the Battle of Passchendaele were reaching their zenith. On 4th October, British infantry over a front of several Corps made an advance at 5.30 a.m. Just previously, the enemy had also advanced and so was caught by both barrages, with the result the number of prisoners taken by the British was very large. The British left reached Poelcappelle and the front came within 2,000 yards of Passchendaele. Because of this advance and the need for extending the light railways, the 2nd Battalion, Canadian Railway Troops, was given more labour from the infantry battalions out at rest. Moving to Flanders on 12th October, to enter the British offensive launched early in June to free the Belgian coast and relieve the French of pressure, the Canadian Corps now entered this fight. Opposite Ypres the trenches ran from Broodseinde to Poelcappelle across bare ridges of clay and marshy hollows drowned by a surfeit of water. Continual rain and the bombardment had turned the fruitful area into an evil quagmire where movement was hazardous. On the 22nd, to anticipate, the 3rd and 4th Canadian Divisions occupied 2,800 yards in the centre of the position with Passchendaele Ridge as their objective; attacked and took Bellevue Spur on the 26th, and four days later reduced Crest Farm and Meetcheele Spur. On 4th and 5th November, the 1st and 2nd Canadian Divisions relieved the 3rd and 4th. Attacking on the 6th they took the Goudberg Spur, Mosselmarkt and Passchendaele and the main ridge overlooking Roulers, making another short advance on the 10th, before returning to the Lens Sector the next week, after a gain of two square miles at a cost of 16,404 casualties. The 2nd C.R.T. never served with the Canadian Corps, but this accomplishment is inserted as the 2nd C.R.T. was to serve nearby while their brother Canadians were in the area and naturally there was contact, and the unit was to be of some service to their own countrymen.

Enemy shelling was so persistent on the 1st and so close to the grade that a party of "A" Company, 2nd C.R.T., and some of the K.O.Y.L.I. unloading ballast on the spur to Wilde Wood had to desist. All empty cars returned carrying wounded, and during the day the wounded were carried to points west of the Canal. A shell break was repaired at Pagoda Corner, two sections being replaced. Work began on a new ammunition refilling point off Morpeth Spur, grading and ditching being done over shell torn country. Heavy firing prevented the repair of a big shell break on the Wilde Wood line, but the night parties repaired several breaks on the Bedlington and other lines nearby between 9 and 10 p.m. Shelling by high velocity guns forced the parties at Vlamertinghe Stone Yard to stop work for two hours that morning. In the evening four battalions attached as labour reported to the unit near the Steel Dump: the 8th King's Own Yorkshire Light Infantry, 2nd Argyll and Sutherland Highlanders, 20th Royal Fusiliers and 10th Duke of Wellington's. That night the maintenance party repaired a break on the Rotherbury line caused by the crossing of tanks, but an effort to repair the Wilde Wood line break was ineffective as the shelling was still too heavy. About 2 a.m. the next night enemy aircraft flew over the rear areas and in the region of Headquarters Camp, Woestenhoek Yard, dropped many large bombs.

Construction parties under Lieuts. Ternan and Smith on the 6th had considerable shelling to contend with and heavy rain also impeded progress. In the region of Pommern Castle shelling was heavy in the morning and again at 2 p.m., seven other ranks of the attached Pioneers and Labour units being killed and six wounded, but the work was pushed steadily forward. The night maintenance party repaired three switches in Woestenhoek Yard and replaced three sections of steel blown by a bomb. Of a draft of 55 reinforcements arriving on the 7th, six failed to pass the medical examination. None of the draft was a railwayman and only 11 had any engineering or mechanical knowledge. Work that day was also hindered by the shelling and heavy rainfall, the country being very hard to cross. Three of the 8th K.O.Y.L.I. were wounded. The rain made grading very hard as the country was a sea of mud, and owing to the poor condition of the roads, many convoys of pack mules carrying field gun ammunition persisted in using the grade. As a result it was in bad condition for laying steel. Delay to traffic was caused at Wieltje while a diamond for a crossing was fitted, and again 400 yards northeast of Mannors Junction, where a 60-pounder gun was loaded on the light railway and removed. That day the unit line reached the Hindenburg Line at Pommern Castle, the ground being cumbered with dead bodies, making the work of grading very unpleasant. The blockhouses also were filled with dead Germans.

Lieut. Ritchie and his working parties laid 100 feet of steel on the 8th in Bedlington opposite the Grey Ruin, and assisted a field battery to move, as the latter was located on the grade. Because of the shelling of Zonnebeke road opposite the site of the work, splinters continually fell among the working parties, but there were no casualties. A break on the Wilde Wood Spur was repaired under heavy shell fire. The heavy rains placed the lines themselves in a serious condition, as in many places mud of the consistency of porridge came over the steel for a depth of 18 inches. Instead of being built too late, the 2nd C.R.T. line was now used by the Artillery General for bringing up ammunition and the material for a plank road. During the night the maintenance party made two repairs, the first delayed by the operating department failing to provide a tractor. The main work on the 9th consisted in keeping the ammunition moving and consolidating lines already built, a difficult task as no ballast could be taken forward from lack of trains and because of the depth of mud everywhere. The shelling became so severe on the Wilde Wood line that the work had to be discontinued at 3 p.m. Shell fire was also prevalent on the Forest Hall line, one of the 2nd Argyll and Sutherland Highlanders being wounded. One party helped to build trench tramways that day, and built a line to the battery at Grey Ruin.

While working with the maintenance party in the night escorting ammunition trains, Spr. W. Leitch was wounded at Mannors Junction by a fragment of a bomb dropped by an enemy aircraft, which flew over the lines and the back areas every night. The 20th Royal Fusiliers were replaced by the 8th King's Own Yorkshire Light Infantry [1] the following day. Work was done on the Wilde Wood Spur salvaging flints to place under the track, which was hourly sinking out of sight in the mud through lack of ballast. In the rain and mud, the party did fine work, raising 500 feet of track. The second shift starting at noon continuing the work rerailed five tractors derailed trying to haul heavy loads over unballasted track and unloaded ammunition wherever necessary. Fencing was completed where required between Pagoda Corner and Grey Ruin on the Bedlington line. Mannors Yard was now complete except for ballasting. The Operating Companies had left cars of ammunition in the Battalion's sidings for days. As these were in the way, Major Gibson collected them, took them up the lines and distributed the shells to battery commanders, "who received them with open arms," as they were running low.

At a conference at Vth Army Headquarters on the 11th, attended by Col. Clarke, it was decided that every aid would be given the Light Railways to consolidate their lines, as their value had been shown in the recent wet weather. Parties of "A" Company, assisting in the unloading of ammunition on Wilde Wood Spur, were heavily shelled near Grey Ruin, and Lieut. Thomas was slightly wounded by a splinter. After his wound was attended to, he resumed his tour of duty. The afternoon shift also came under shell fire for an hour and a half, during which time work was stopped, and the same party was shelled again on their way back to camp between Wilde Wood and Oxford road, one other rank of the 20th Royal Fusiliers being killed and two wounded. "C" Company at Watou Camp was inspected by Col. Clarke the following day. In Woestenhoek Yards 200 feet of steel blown the previous night was replaced. Three Simplex tractors were allotted to the unit that day to operate for construction work. A quantity of stove pipe secured for the stoves made from oil drums in the machine shop was welcomed, as the frequent early morning frosts made stoves a luxury. The Headquarters officers moved from their tent into a hut covered with roofing material and renovated. The next

---

(1) An infantry unit; the 12th K.O.Y.L.I. were Pioneers.

day the work consisted of improving and consolidating all lines and helping to move the ammunition forward.

A car loaded with 9.2-inch shells left on the main line near the Lace Factory caused a collision and derailment in the night, so the ammunition was transferred to another car; the derailed car put on the line, and the latter cleared. On the Bedlington line 192 feet of steel was laid and a switch installed, completing the passing siding near Grey Ruin, and so facilitating the clearance of traffic for the Wilde Wood line, on which timber was salvaged to place under the track, the only possible means of laying the line open for traffic owing to the lack of ballast. On the Morpeth line the working party had one casualty, when on taking shelter in a dugout in a severe shower, Spr. C. Lavigne accidentally touched a live Mills bomb, which exploded, wounding him. It was supposed that the excessive dampness had rusted the pin almost in two and the effect of the kick broke it. Twice on the 14th fleets of enemy aircraft passed over the Battalion camp and dropped bombs over the area and in the evening an observation balloon was brought down in flames by a German aircraft using phosphorus bullets.

The arrival of the Canadian Corps in the area, of which rumour had spoken for some days, was hailed with enthusiasm by the 2nd C.R.T., as it was the first time the unit had worked with the Corps since arrival in France. Enemy shell fire the following afternoon hindered work of laying steel, lifting and ballasting in the Bedlington extension. In the evening the usual enemy bombing by aircraft occurred near Culloden, Spr. McIlroy being wounded in the forehead by a bomb splinter. Col. Clarke attended a conference at Canadian Corps Headquarters at Ten Elms Camp. In laying steel on the Bedlington line, as the grade was very wet it was necessary to put planks under the steel ties on the 16th. A party of the 20th Royal Fusiliers grading forward had to return because of the shelling, so they worked salvaging timber for that purpose. Until enough was collected, the steel party stayed in the neighbouring trenches as several shells landed on either side of the grade. Ballasting then started at Grey Ruin, but it was evident that the enemy had the parties under observation, as he advanced his fire and the shells dropped close to the ballasting parties. One train of four cars had been unloaded and was pulling out when a truck was derailed. This had just been rerailed when a shell landed 90 yards away, breaking the line behind it, and alighting only six feet from another party hauling sand, but the crew escaped injury. Work was ordered stopped, as the observation was perfect. The shelling continued, eight falling in Grey Ruin siding in five minutes, breaking the line in six places. Direct hits were made on a tractor, a car of steel and a car of bridging material, the tractor being switched round at right angles to the track, but although the shelling continued all afternoon there were no casualties. Lance Corporal Eastwood of "A" Company coolly directed the work while the shells were falling within 15 yards from him. A party replacing steel at a break near Wilde Wood switch was shelled off the work twice. On the Rotherbury line six sections of broken steel were replaced. Shelling was also heavy near the work all day in the "B" Company area on the Forest Hall line.

An attempt to clear the wreckage at Grey Ruin siding the following morning was unsuccessful, as the shell fire was still too heavy. In the afternoon it was quieter and all construction cars were cleared, but the line was still blocked by the tractor, which the Operating Company had not moved. Spr. G.H. Yeomans was wounded on the Rotherbury line by a fragment of a shell, which landed about 300 yards away. Canadian Corps units encamping around the Advance Camp near Ypres made it seem like old Camp Borden days in Canada at this time. The afternoon party the next day narrowly escaped a large bombing raid near Grey Ruin and the Zonnebeke road, and assisted four other ranks of the 6th C.R.T. wounded by a bomb near Wilde Wood Switch. Plans were made that day for special efforts on the Gravenstafel line. Two other ranks of the 1st Lincolns, attached as labour, were wounded by shell fragments. In the afternoon in a hostile air raid, a bomb dropped near "B" Company's Camp, seriously wounding six other ranks of the 12th/13th Northumberland Fusiliers. Early in the afternoon two enemy aircraft were brought down by machine gun fire near Culloden Camp.

Although the wet weather continued unabated, the unit's animals were in dry, weathertight stables, and each man was given a third blanket, as the damp nights were very trying. Shelling in the Forest Hall line became so heavy that the parties there had to cease work at 4 p.m. on the 19th. The following day the Assistant Director of Light Railways, IInd Army, took over the system of light railways, including Woestenhoek Yards, from the A.D.L.R. Vth Army. In working on the Gravenstafel line, wooden ties were now being used in place of steel ties, as the latter did not give enough bearing surface in the sea of mud. That afternoon, Lance-Corporal P.L. Burrell was seriously wounded, and one other rank killed and two of the 1st Sherwood Foresters wounded by a shell bursting close to the work. A draft of three Officers, Lieuts. E.R. Vigor, G.S. Perry and J.C.R. McPherson arrived from the C.R.T. Depot, Purfleet, on the 21st, and Lieut. G.O. Thomas of "A" Company became mechanical engineer at Battalion Headquarters in charge of the machine shop and mechanical transport. Working parties, including attached labour, were driven off their work on the Gravenstafel line in the afternoon by high explosive shells. When that ceased, the ballast party resumed unloading, but were again driven off by low overhead shrapnel. Enemy aircraft again dropped bombs in the vicinity of Culloden Camp.

The 5th Provisional Cavalry Pioneer Battalion [2], consisting of personnel from the Life Guards, Dragoon Guards, Hussars, Royal Canadian Dragoons, Lord Strathcona's Horse, Fort Garry Horse, 9th Hudson Horse, 8th Bengal Lancers, 17th Lancers and Essex Yeomanry, reported for duty to the 2nd C.R.T. the following day. At 10.45 a.m. the grading and steel parties on the Gravenstafel line were shelled off the work, and before they got clear a high explosive shell exploded among them, causing 15 casualties. Three of the 12th King's Own Yorkshire Light Infantry Pioneers were killed and ten wounded and Sprs. T. Williams and J. Maher of "A" Company, 2nd C.R.T., were wounded, the latter remaining on duty. He and L/Cpl. J.W. Garton of the K.O.Y.L.I. led in assisting the other

---

[2] Commanded by Lt.-Col. Douglas Young.

wounded.(3) That morning "B" Company moved forward to a new camp site near Wieltje, where it was necessary to build everything, as there were neither dugouts nor shelters. On the Gravenstafel line the next day the parties had to face considerable shell fire. The steel party was unable to do anything, but the grading party worked with shells dropping 200 yards away. At 3.30 p.m. the enemy shortened his range and several shells burst alongside the party, but its members were saved as the soft mud prevented fragmentation, although the work had to be stopped after 600 feet was graded. The party of Lieut. Draper grading on the Bridge House Spur was also driven away.

The enemy was particularly active most of the day forward of Bridge House, but despite this a party with a tractor pulled another tractor out of a shell hole on the track south of Pommern Castle, but were prevented from repairing two breaks east of that point. Grading on the road to Gravenstafel was practically impossible, but a little ditching and draining was done by small, isolated parties. Credit was given Lieuts. Bonn and Ewing for their example and judgment in advancing the work a little at a time. On the Gravenstafel line on the 24th 500 feet of the forward grade was rebuilt and 480 feet of steel laid and partially ballasted. A car of steel which had been ditched was salvaged and used, and one bad break requiring six lengths, and two bridges settling were also repaired. One of the 192nd Labour Company in St. Jean was killed by enemy fire. In the afternoon shift "B" Company's work ahead of Bridge House was interrupted and stopped by intermittent shell fire, Beck House line being particularly subject to enemy attention. It was impossible to repair all the breaks between Pommern Castle and Beck House, but two of 25 feet diameter and 12 feet deep were repaired and the line cleared past the battery requiring ammunition.

As the result of heavy shelling, two breaks occurred 100 yards south of Spree Farm, and a volunteer party consisting of Cpl. Reid and five men of "B" Company under Capt.

---

(3) M.M. *London Gazette* 2.4.18.

Adams repaired them. They were shelled off just as the work neared completion, a shell alighting a yard from the track helping derail the tool car of the breakdown train, but this was remedied later. The party had to run the gauntlet of shells for 200 yards, but escaped without casualties. As a result of the bombing one of the attached labour units had one man killed and one wounded on the Wieltje line. At 5.30 p.m. the enemy started promiscuous firing in the direction of the Battalion Headquarters Camp, but the heavy wind and rain caused the shells to fall short.

On the Gravenstafel line on the 25th the work party was driven off at 2 p.m. by shell fire, which continued all afternoon. Work around Spree Farm was also interrupted by shell fire and the party had to replace seven cars on the track, the train having been blown. Before the break was repaired, 40 feet of steel was necessary to remedy another break. Lieut. Draper became Quartermaster the following day, when the lines in the forward area were busy bringing down the wounded from Bridge House, about 500 in all being carried over the Battalion's system. "A" and "D" Companies of the 12th K.O.Y.L.I. Pioneers arrived from the St. Jean Camp at the site of the old "C" Company Camp at Culloden in pouring rain, and it was nearly dark when all were settled in the new quarters in Nissen Huts, luxury itself compared with the old sandbag shelters at St. Jean.

Steel was laid over three repaired breaks on the Forest Hall line and two shell holes were filled and another large break repaired. Ballast was carried forward to Spree Farm and two cars were dumped at Bridge House Collecting Station, the returning empty trains bringing back wounded. While the two trains were being loaded there, the enemy shelled both sides of the track near Rat Farm, breaking it in one place and grazing it in another. While Capt. Adams and a party aided by six German prisoners filled the shell hole and temporarily repaired the break, Lieut. Ewing twice rerailed a tractor. Shells began to fall just short of the party, so the prisoners pushed the cars of wounded beyond the danger zone. It was then possible to get the tractor across the spot and then a second hospital train, the only incidents being one man blown into a ditch, a dump burnt and a tractor burnt and struck in six places.

The track was remedied an hour and a half later, and two trains of ammunition reached their destination only half an hour late. That morning "C" Company took over the St. Jean camp from "A", and during the day Watou Camp closed, as all four companies had each enjoyed a period there. "B" Company moved camp to White Pole Corner the next day and began building splinter-proof shelters.

As the recreation hut had been blown up in the past week, a church service was held in the Headquarters Officers' mess on the 28th, Capt. T.G. McGonigle, formerly Chaplain of the 127th Battalion, taking the service in the absence of Capt. Allan. The cars hauling ballast to Forest Hall line returned carrying wounded from the dressing station at Bridge House, about 300 being moved. In the afternoon the usual bombing raid occurred. The next evening shells and bombs fell near the camp at St. Jean, spattering the dugouts with debris. Trains returning from Bridge House carried wounded that day and on the next five trains of wounded were hauled in the morning and in the afternoon and night two cars and a tractor continued with the work. Three breaks from aerial bombs were repaired. Rowland Hill, Canadian Press Correspondent, visited the Battalion on the 31st, meeting Col. Clarke at St. Jean. A Hallowe'en dinner was given in the officers' mess at which Col. Clarke presented a cup and medal to Spr. John Hopper and a medal to Spr. A. Free for sports events. On behalf of the Canadian Corps Commander, Brig.-Gen. G.F. Farmer forwarded to the Battalion a letter from the Officer Commanding the 186th Siege Battery, Royal Garrison Artillery, for assistance voluntarily rendered by the 2nd C.R.T. when the battery was having great difficulty in getting ammunition up to its gun positions at Spree Farm. In particular, Lieut. J.T. Jenkins' "services were invaluable."

On 1st November, the unit was advised that the name of the Forest Hall line had been revised to Forest Hill; Pommern line instead of Forest Hall, and Y-6 instead of Gravenstafel. The spur for guns at Bridge House was to be known as Y-7 and the new line to the east as Y-8. As it was dull the usual bombing raids by enemy aircraft failed to materialize. One trip was made to Mannors from Bridge

House with wounded. Because of shelling, the parties from Wieltje Camp in the afternoon had to be withdrawn, and sent to the Forest Hill line to surface. Word was received the following day that Lieut. Brunton, an original officer of the unit, who had transferred to the 75th Battalion and won the Military Cross, was killed two days previously on Abr'am Heights near Passchendaele. Lieuts. D.C. Wills, F. Clarke, W.A. Macdonald and E. Smith arrived from Purfleet; all had practical engineering experience. A party on the Forest Hill line diversion lifting and ballasting was shelled off the work, one of the K.O.Y.L.I. and one of the 5th Provisional Cavalry Pioneer Battalion being wounded. Owing to shelling the next day, "D" Company and attached labour stopped work, Sprs. T.E. Coggins and E. Inger being wounded by shrapnel.

At 4.45 a.m. on the 4th, the night party of "A" Company repaired line at Atherley Junction broken by a high velocity shell. A party of "C" Company in the afternoon was shelled off the work at Carnation Dump. On the Pommern line shelling was also fairly heavy and the parties were several times driven off temporarily. One other rank of the Royal Canadian Dragoons and six of the Bengal Lancers were wounded. On the Forest Hill line the following day, Spr. McRae was wounded while in a train on the forward line. After the 1st and 2nd Canadian Divisions went over the top at daylight on the 6th and gaining their objectives, taking new positions to about 400 yards past Passchendaele Village, the enemy's counter-barrage seriously interfered with work on the forward line of the 2nd C.R.T., especially Y-8 and the Pommern line, necessitating the temporary cessation of work. In the afternoon empties returning from the forward area carried wounded to Mannors Junction, in all about 40. Shelling that day was severe on the crossover to Canadian Corps tramway and on the Y-6 line, Spr. K.T. McLeod being wounded by shrapnel and Spr. L. Malette shell shocked, and in addition 11 other ranks of the Cavalry unit and one of the 12th K.O.Y.L.I. were wounded. On the Pommern line the ballasting party had to stop work at 10 a.m. because of the shelling, moving to the Wieltje Diversion. Another party on the Pommern line dug 1,000 feet of offtake ditches before the shelling compelled them to stop, after which they moved to the Forest Hill line and dug another 1,000 feet there. About 30 wounded were taken from Iberian House on the Y-8 line to the Bridge House Dressing Station.

The following day the grade on the Canadian Corps tram line was completed and 900 feet of steel laid, rendering it fit for traffic when ballasted. Shelling was continuous in the locality during the day. More wounded were brought from Bridge House in the empties that day, and in the evening bombs were dropped over White Pole Camp. More shelling was experienced the next day on the cross over to Canadian Corps line, but there were no casualties. On the Y-8 line parties ballasted 100 feet and graded that distance before being driven by shell fire to the Canadian Corps tram line to lay steeel. Another party of "D" Company and K.O.Y.L.I. was ditching on this line and was shelled. Sgt. W.J. Hyett was killed and Sprs. H. Siegel and O.G. Wright wounded, while the K.O.Y.L.I. had three other ranks killed and five wounded. The party was taken off for the rest of the shift. Sgt. Hyett was buried in the afternoon at the British Military Cemetery at Nine Elms with military honours. Shelling was again general in the White Pole Corner sector on the 10th, Spr. N.V. Richardson being wounded, and the shelling was also frequent during the night. On the Canadian Corps tramway line, "D" Company and some of the K.O.Y.L.I. put in a switch, spiked track, placed 200 feet of guard rail on a curve and ballasted 500 feet with sand. Four breaks from shell fire were repaired, and the party found shelling very heavy, Spr. Davies being wounded.

Shelling near White Pole Corner was heavy all the following day. An enemy aircraft coming over the Woestenhoek Yard at 9 p.m. and returning along the Elverdinghe Road dropped bombs on both, one dropping in the transport lines, killing Spr. W. Bouchard and wounding five other ranks. In an air raid the next day over the Ypres region, several bombs were dropped in St. Jean yard, one wounding Spr. P.J. Harding. At night there was much air activity near White Pole and shell also dropped close to the camp there. German aircraft were, in fact, very active all day, several bombs dropping close to "B" Company's camp early in the morning and again at 11 a.m. One shell landing in the camp luckily exploded in a ditch. One of the King's Regiment working with "D" Company was seriously wounded by a bomb. On the ensuing evening the usual shelling in the region of White Pole camp occurred, several falling near the dugouts. On the 18th an enemy aircraft attacked and sent a British observation balloon down in flames in the White Pole area, and the parties on the Pommern line were three times shelled off work. Spr. G. Cade was slightly wounded on the following day. Comments the diarist: "Credit is due Cpl. E. Mills and L/Cpl. W. Kyle, who have on several trying occasions during the last few days acted with great coolness and courage, carrying on with their duties while under shell fire, and by their example helping the parties to complete the work."

Parties of "A" Company laying steel, ballasting and grading on Y-6 (Gravenstafel) line on the 20th were unable to work after 2.45 p.m., as repeated salvoes came from enemy artillery, the shells exploding within a 10 to 30-foot radius, but owing to the softness of the ground there were no casualties. About 9 p.m. the camp at White Pole was liberally shelled with high explosive, five other ranks being wounded, and considerable damage done to the camp, one hut being demolished and a hole drilled in the orderly room of "B" Company by a piece of shell. Two platoons of "A" Company the following day at Culloden had to move to another part of the line on account of the severe shell fire. A part of "D" Company and King's Liverpool Regiment attempted to work on the Pommern line the next day, but were stopped by shell fire, Spr. J. Latimer of "D" Company and one other rank of the King's being wounded. Late on the next afternoon an enemy aircraft came overhead near White Pole Camp, dropping a bomb, which injured some Imperial troops nearby. Called to Hagle to repair a shell break, the night party was shelled off twice before finally clearing the line.

In two sections, the Battalion left the Ypres area by train for Doullens on the 27th for a month's rest in billets. On arrival, half of Headquarters details and "A" and "B" Companies under Major Holdsworth marched to Mezerolles, where the Headquarters and "B" Company were to be billeted, arriving at 3.45 a.m. "A" was billeted with the transport at Remaisnil about two miles away. "C" and "D" Companies were located in Mezerolles, and two mornings later in that town all ranks were wakened by the almost forgotten strains of the Battalion bugle and trumpet band, and resorted to drill, physical training and a reduced scale of rations. The personnel of the unit remarked on the reasonableness and tolerance of the French of this area. On 2nd December the bugle and brass bands played the unit to the field off the Mezerolles-Remaisnil road, and the latter played for Divine service, conducted by Hon. Capt. Allan. Voting in the Dominion Election (this resulted in the return of the Union Government) started the next day, continuing until the 17th, Capt. Flood being deputy returning officer for Headquarters, Lieut. Ternan for "A" Company, Capt. Adams for "B", Major Craig for "C" and Lieut. Galbraith for "D" Company. The Canadian Y.M.C.A. provided two gramophones, two libraries and varied games, as well as a marquee. A lorry service was organized from Chimney Corner, Mezerolles, to Doullens, and the number of personnel entitled to leave to England was slightly increased. Headquarters office huts were erected and an officers' mess went under construction, built from three wooden huts and capable of accommodating all officers of the unit. "A" Company defeated the 9th C.R.T. at football on the 4th. Good weather and fine cross-country tracks impelled the officers to ride, and that day a party went through the woods behind Remaisnil Chateau, belonging to a local mine owner.

The Battalion Signals by the following day had a complete line of communication between Battalion Headquarters and Army Signals, Doullens, and to the various companies. A new bandmaster, Drum Major H. Somerville, originally of the 12th Regiment, York Rangers [4], who had come overseas with the 4th Battalion, arrived from the General Base, Etaples. The brass band now boasted 23 players and the bugle and trumpet band under Sgt. Vincent 28. On the evening of the 6th, the officers attended a dinner at No. 3 Canadian Stationary Hospital, Doullens. Frevent

---

(4) Parent unit of the 2nd C.R.T.

was soon included in the lorry service as well as Doullens. Battalion drill, musketry instruction and route marches and a class of instruction and lectures for officers recently joined featured the training programme. Maj.-Gen. Nash inspected the unit on the 14th. A concert was given by the concert party of the 3rd Canadian Stationary Hospital in the recreation tent near Chimney Corner, and another on Christmas Eve by the officers of the Battalion. The second Christmas away from home was celebrated in the traditional manner, the brass band touring both towns in the morning and giving a concert of carols. Each Company had a special dinner, the several menus consisting of roast pig, roast beef, several vegetables and for dessert plum pudding of Government recipe and of the unit's own.

CHAPTER VIII

BEAUMETZ AND CUGNY

Orders were received on 2nd January, 1918, for one company of the 2nd Battalion, Canadian Railway Troops, to entrain at Doullens the next day for Tincourt to take over the Marquaix Yard and construct lines leading out of Tincourt. The remainder of the unit was to move to Bouvincourt and Beaumetz, and "B" Company, selected to go to Tincourt, entrained as instructed on the 3rd. "A" and "C" Companies entrained the following day for the Vth Army area by way of Tincourt railhead. A party of the unit marched to the cinema, where 1916 recruiting films of the unit were shown, before the train left Doullens. "B" Company, arriving at Tincourt on the 4th, were accommodated in two Adrian Huts without floors and liable to flooding. "A" and "C" Company reached Tincourt the following day, "A" being housed in Bouvincourt and "C" in Beaumetz. The survey party of "A" Company immediately began the location of the line from Hancourt to connect the British with the French system at Beauvois. With headquarters established in a school house, the men of the company were billeted in two large lofts over stables, and 30-hundredweight of dry straw obtained from the Corps Agricultural Officer enabled the men to make themselves very comfortable. The town was a German Headquarters prior to evacuation and not badly battered.

"C" Company Camp of Nissen huts lay in the garden of a former Chateau, before the enemy destroyed it in his withdrawal. Well protected from the wind by a high brick wall, its huts were neatly arranged with walks of duckboard along which in summer flowers and shrubs had been planted. Recently it had been occupied by a French unit, which left it in a dirty condition, and removed nearly all the matchboarding for firewood. By sealing all gaps in the wall and lining the interior with tar paper, however, a comfortable camp was established, and there was an abundance of wood from shattered buildings and trees felled by the enemy. Battalion Headquarters, "D" Company and the transport arrived by train early on the 6th. While waiting to start they had been bombed by hostile aircraft and Sprs. R. Graham and J. Fraser were wounded by splinters and taken to Peronne Hospital. Headquarters went to Beaumetz and "D" Company and the transport to Bouvincourt. Headquarters was located in Nissen huts adjoining "C" Company, the men also occupying numerous dugouts and cellars in the grounds in preference to huts, which in the present severe weather were cold and draughty. "D" Company moved into Santin Farm, Headquarters of the 3rd Dismounted Cavalry Division. "B" Company and the technical stores took over the light railway yard at Marquaix to put it in order, which was needed badly, as ties, switches, rails and sides of cars were all jumbled together and the whole buried under several train loads of cinder ballast.

Besides the line from Hancourt to Beauvois to complete, to facilitate the transfer of rolling stock from the British to the French system, a line for the Cavalry Corps from Flamicourt was required near Peronne to join the former line near Vraignes. A standard gauge yard was being built about 100 yards down the old metre gauge line from Flamicourt to be joined to Estrées and entailing careful work in projecting a location over the canal. On the 7th Lieut. McIlwraith marched a party to the yard on the light railway between Hancourt and Vraignes to receive material and establish a yard for storing construction material for the Hancourt-Beauvois line. Heavy fog and intermittent snow storms hampered the work of the survey party on the Hancourt-Beauvois line. That day a Y.M.C.A. library and reading room for the use of "D" Company was installed in Bouvincourt. Two survey parties working from either end of the line mentioned connected the following day and that night the plan and profile were completed and forwarded. Each company ("A", "C" and "D") was allotted a definite section of the line. To save time, all switches received were laid out, the parts fitted and earmarked. The percentage of switches fitting together was now high and bore evidence of greater care in manufacture. When the previous day's snow storms turned to rain and it thawed, general thaw precautions were put in force on the roads, so all movement of material by horse or motor transport came to a halt.

Work on the Hancourt-Beauvois line began on the 10th, with grading and laying steel, in addition to receiving and unloading material. Lieut. W.A. McDonald and 43 other ranks cleared bush and began grading along the sunken road, heaviest piece of work in "A" Company's section. A heavy cut made more difficult by cavalry crossing it on a horse transport track which had trampled it was repaired. "B" Company survey party under Lieut. Graham moved into tents near Tertry to place themselves nearer their work, while the remainder of the Company continued clearing Marquaix Yard. On the following night, the unit was advised that it would take over construction on the line to Epehy to meet the 12th Battalion, Canadian Railway Troops, the distance for the time being 1,500 yards. The work became the responsibility of "B" Company. The 59th Labour Company, R.E., loaned the unit, was detailed to "A" Company on the 14th, when "B" Company began work on the proposed line to Epehy, until word was received that the line had been abandoned. First used by the 2nd C.R.T. the following day, a supply of an explosive known as "Blastine" was found to be quicker than blasting powder, but not as powerful as dynamite, although a satisfactory substitute. Good results were obtained in shattering tree trunks by placing several sticks on the bole covered by a layer of mud.

"B" Company was warned to move to Le Mesnil, where on the 16th Lieut. Graham and the survey party retraced the line of the old metre gauge, Flamicourt-Mons. Lieuts. Ritchie and Draper began the location of the line to Mons-en-Chaussée two days later, staking 4,700 feet before rain stopped the work, but it was completed the next day. The following day the unit was advised that the Army had asked for the Hancourt-Beauvois line to be completed by 15th February, and were sending a large force of labour for the purpose. In the afternoon Major Gibson drove to Trefçon to arrange for the movement of "D" Company and place the latter under canvas there near their section of work and thence to the end of the line. Two companies of Indian labour, the 70th and 79th Command Companies reported on the 21st. At the time and before the end of the month, the 32nd, 33rd, 90th and 74th Labour Companies, R.E., were also attached. "D" Company was ordered to move to Trefçon that day, and on the next the Battalion received a draft of 64 from the Depot, Purfleet. By the 24th it turned out that some of the new draft had measles, so those at Tincourt were quarantined and also any of the remainder who had been sent to Le Mesnil.

Army now requested the completion of the Hancourt-Beauvois line by 5th February, or ten days in advance of the original date. "B" Company moved from Tincourt to Le Mesnil on the 25th, when the Brie line was located. Steel was now being laid on the Hancourt line, while grading, trimming and ditching continued, and on the Mons line grading. By the 27th, steel was being laid on the Mons-en-Chaussée line, although the work was held up temporarily owing to a very large cut to be removed. Steel was started on the Flamicourt-Mons line the following day. The promotions of Captains Adams and Greenlees to the rank of major and Lieuts. Graham and Galbraith to that of captain were published. Lieut. Graham was also appointed Acting Major and Lieut. Ternan Acting Captain.

A bridge on the Hancourt-Beauvois line and the steel laying there were completed on 1st February by the placing of a siding and two switches. Grading the new Brie line was commenced, 360 feet of heavy fill being completed. New artillery stables opposite the camp at Le Mesnil aroused disquiet, as they would destroy the view and attract hostile aircraft. "D" Company was given responsibility for the maintenance of the French lines at Foreste, so an advance party of 25 other ranks left that day. The Army asked all units who would to plant potatoes, so profiting by its experience at the farm at Velu the previous summer, the Battalion asked for ten acres to cultivate. On the 3rd advice came that Italian labour would be attached, and the 64th and 65th Italian Labour Companies arrived shortly. The Hancourt-Beauvois line, 5¾ miles long, was completed on the 4th as far as connecting steel was concerned, a day ahead of the date set by the Army, a result especially satisfactory as so many difficulties were presented by the formation and topography of the country. On the line were three bridges, one trestle bridge being unique in that it was the longest built for light railways in France. From 10 to 12 feet high, it was 285 feet in length.

One of the other bridges crossing a fairly deep river had a single span of 15 feet and a height of 11 feet, while the third bridge, in "D" Company's section, ran over a re-entrant and was made up of several bents over a total span of 40 feet with a height of 12 feet. As the location led through a country of hills covered with bush, the section between Tertry and just south of Trefçon presented many difficulties. The line was nothing but a series of cuts and fills, much of it being side hill work, and in some places the fill had been shored up with facines built of twigs. The steel was largely the ordinary 60-centimetre rail, but in places the old metre track was used. The only ties were of wood, metre ties being placed about every third tie for additional bearing. On this line that day, "D" Company laid 6,000 feet of steel by 4 p.m.

Calling upon Col. Clarke on the evening of the 6th, the Baron Marcette explained that the 64th and 65th Italian Labour Companies were composed of men who had been wounded, and so in the eyes of their Government need not again return to the front line. The following day work in the transshipment yard at Flamicourt began. Inspecting the Hancourt line on the 10th, the Deputy Director of Light Railways expressed his approval of it and of the trestles and other bridges. "C" Company moved that day to Flavy-le-Martel to billets in damaged houses, with Headquarters in a building occupied by the area commandant. On the latter date, "B" Company completed the Mons-en-Chaussée line for 2,150 feet, with the exception of fish plates, while 1,500 feet of grading was done on the Brie line. Battalion Headquarters moved from Beaumetz to Cugny the following day, when "C" Company was ordered to begin work the next day on the transshipping point at Flavy-le-Martel. "A" Company tried hard to complete its section of the Mons-en-Chaussée line, as it was moving the next day, but the lack of fish plates prevented finishing the last 100 feet of track. On the 15th, the unit was asked by Army to complete the Brie line by the 19th ("B Company) and that "C" Company finish ammunition refilling points at Flavy-le-Martel and Villers-St. Christophe by the next day. "A" Company moved by motor lorry to Chauny. In an air raid the following day, Spr. H. Aley was wounded at Chauny by a splinter, the blast shattering many windows in the officers' quarters.

At Cugny the Headquarters offices were built in the courtyard of the farm. The main house was used for the Commanding Officer's quarters and officers' mess, and the other buildings around the square for men's billets, although the majority were housed in huts built by their former occupants, the French, in a large field to the south. The transport was placed in many stables about the farm. Without exception, those were the most comfortable quarters Battalion Headquarters had had, the only drawback being the lack of good drinking water, which had to be hauled from a water point in Flavy-le-Martel. At one end of the courtyard was a pond filled with fish before the war, but then practically a cess pool, because of the way it was used by the Germans, who lived there for about two years. They removed all the fish and filled the pond with garbage. Spr. J.W. Morrison of "A" Company was killed and Cpl. E. Riding, Cpl. H. Eastwood and Spr. E.T. Gray were wounded on the evening of the 17th when a bomb from an enemy aircraft fell outside one of the billets. The raid lasted from 7 until 9 p.m. Two days later the remainder of "D" Company moved to Foreste to join its detached party.

During the month a large number of repairs to Battalion equipment, such as water tanks, stoves and motorcycles, were made in the workshop, in charge of Capt. Thomas. Bolts used recently on bridges were also made and a boiler capable of heating water for a bath house salvaged and repaired. Experiments with a view to building standard huts from corrugated iron were made and a sample hut was under construction. For maintenance purposes the line at Flavy-le-Martel was divided into areas on the 25th: No. 1 from Avesnes to Benay, with the party billeted at Montescourt-Lizerolles; No. 2 from Bois de Frières to Hinacourt, billeted at Frières-Faillouel; No. 3 from Bois de Frières to Villette, billeted at Villaquier-Aumont. Each party of ten was under a corporal, the labour being supplied by the 61st Labour Company, R.E. No. 11 Platoon of "C" Company went by lorry to start on the Nesle-Voyennes line and were billeted in Manicourt, where the 1st Entrenching Battalion was allotted for labour. On the last day of the month, arrangements were made for the Battalion to maintain the XVIIIth and IIIrd Corps areas to bring the lines into good shape in the event of the expected enemy offensive, which actually was launched in less than a month. Five tractors were to be allotted, and with each a flat well car. "A" Company was to have one tractor at the Abbecourt Stone siding; "C" one at Bois Frières and another at Flavy Royal Engineers siding and "D" one at Germaine and another at Pithon Junction. The Flamicourt-Mons line was completed ready to be turned over to the 12th C.R.T. that day.

A new medical officer, 1st Lieut. A. Button of the United States Reserve, was attached to the unit for duty on 1st March to replace Major Gauthier, who had succeeded Major R.M. Hillary. On this date the diarist comments: "Last night was supposed to have been the time of the great enemy offensive. It seems that we are the only unit in the locality that has not packed up for any emergency that might arise. It is said that the 'wind' is vertical in 'No Man's Land'." Major Graham and Lieut. Ritchie reconnoitred the line from Appilly to Noyon that day. On the Ham-Noyon line the old metre gauge grade was cleared for 4,800 feet and also 2,500 feet near Ham on the boulevard to get connection with the light railway at the town, but this work was rendered useless by the change in plans of the Assistant Director of Light Railways, who decided to take off from the standard gauge on the Ham-Voyennes line. Major Graham and a survey party located a line from Ham Junction to the Canal at Pithon Wood to join the existing light railway.

The D.A. and Q.M.G., Fifth Army, under date of 2nd March, wrote the Assistant Director-General to ask him to inform the Officer Commanding "B" Company, 2nd C.R.T., (Major Adams) of his high appreciation of the work recently performed with the assistance of the 90th British Labour Company and the 70th Kumaon Indian Labour Company. By the close cooperation of all ranks of all three companies, it was possible to lay 18,200 feet of steel in five days, averaging 3,640 feet a day, the maximum laid in one day being 6,500 feet, a figure which easily held the record in France. The D.A. and Q.M.G. said further that he was also to draw attention to the fact that this feat in track-laying had been performed by a truly Imperial working party, consisting as it did of personnel from Canada, Great Britain and India. "This splendid Imperial co-operation adds a unique feature to the performance, which reflects (the) greatest credit on all concerned," he added.

At the Church parade of Battalion Headquarters at Cugny on the 23rd, a detachment of the Young Citizens Volunteers from Belfast attended. The next day Lieut. T.J. Jenkins of "B" Company left for England to report to the Admiralty, as he had received an appointment under the Imperial Inventions Board. "D" Company, still at Foreste, with labour from the 14th Royal Irish Fusiliers and 83rd Labour Company, made surveys, laid 1,600 feet of steel and ballasted and did 3,600 feet of lining and some maintenance. On the Brie line the next day, 4,705 feet of steel was laid and full tied and spiked by "B" Company and the 65th Italian Labour Company. The steel was hauled in the night from the Flamicourt Yard, saving much time, with two tractors and four flat cars. There was considerable trouble with the 20 horse power tractors owing to the quantity of water in the gasoline. On the Ham-Noyon line, 1,800 feet of grade was cleared and the grade already cleared trimmed but because of failure to secure permission to bridge several large craters, these had to be filled. The survey of the Ham-Noyon line, 13.4 miles, was completed, and "C" Company survey party located the revision of the line Curchy on the Omiecourt-Nesle-Voyennes line. Major Gibson and Lieut. Muir took two tractors and five flat cars by lorry from the yard of the 22nd Operating Company near Ham (Sebastopol) to "C" Company's line near Dreslincourt, northwest of Nesle. The following day on the Brie line 3,900 feet of steel was laid, but no work could be done on the Somme bridges owing to the non-arrival of the pile drivers. At Foreste repairs to the line were made between that town and Auroir, 1,425 feet between Foreste and Villecholles, 660 feet between Foreste and Pithon and 1,110 feet between the latter and Artemps, and 870 feet between that place and Oestres.

Work on the main road east of the Somme on the 7th was hampered by the great piles of rubbish through which a 7-foot cut was necessary, but from Station 62 west of the Somme River, 375 feet of steel was laid and track material distributed for the next day's work. The handling of material from the Brie Yard was simplified by the loan of ten lorries from the Cavalry Corps. The rain that night put the French line in Bois Frières in a very bad state, and when Major Gibson went to investigate the next day he found that the fish plates they used were very light and so when the British rolling stock went over them a shearing action resulted. On the Brie line 2,340 feet of grading was done near Assevillers by "B" Company and the 86th Labour Company. On the line at the first bridge crossing the Somme, it was necessary to move several large tree stumps in the centre of the grade. Steel laying was limited by lack of tractors and rolling stock, but five flat cars were "secured" and hauled over the Somme bridge on the road behind a lorry, and with their aid 2,971 feet were laid on the Ham-Noyon line. On the Ham-Voyennes line 3,000 feet of steel was laid and full spiked. On these jobs were parties of "B" Company and the 11th Durham Light Infantry. The survey party under Major Graham completed the survey to Cugny, more than five miles. On the Omiecourt-Nesle-Voyennes line parties of "C" Company and the 25th Entrenching Battalion (2nd/8th Royal Warwickshire Regiment) did 1,300 feet of grading, and 1,500 feet of ballast was removed from the old metre gauge.

Hon. Capt. Allen held a Church parade on the 10th of Headquarters details with the Warwicks in the open between Cugny and Flavy-le-Martel with the brass band in attendance. The pile driver required for the Somme bridges was finally located at Mesnil. The next day on the west end of the Brie-Estrées line 2,000 feet of grading was done and 3,600 feet of steel laid, despite difficulties with the tractors. Although these had been overhauled, both were without fan belts. Several minor road crossings were placed and a large one over the Peronne-Amiens road, the latter very difficult because of the intense traffic. Bridge material offloaded in the Brie Yard was taken to the bridge site over the Somme, where the pile driver was finally placed. To facilitate the distribution of steel along the canal line, the use of a barge and two French sailors were secured the following day from the French Commandant de Marine. "B" Company's survey party completed the proposed line from Villeselve to Flavy-le-Martel. Army Signals removed telegraph poles in the way at the Somme crossing on the 13th. General Hambro of Fifth Army expressed great satisfaction over the work done on the various lines the next day. He inspected all lines from Brie, Flamicourt, Mons, Tertry to Ham, and saw the driving of the first pile of the Somme bridge crossing. The second bent of the east bridge was driven the following day, and stringers were placed temporarily to allow that track to be carried over it.

All Companies specialized on steel laying to break the present record of 5½ miles a day on the 16th. As far as possible no previous preparations were made beyond getting as much material to hand as possible, the demand generally exceeding the supply. "A" Company on the Chauny-Noyon line laid 12,211 feet of steel, with 75 of the 2nd C.R.T. and 68 unskilled labourers in six hours, completing 14.2 feet a man hour in 858 man hours of work. "B" Company on the Brie-Fay line laid 6,396 feet with 30 of their own men and 166 labourers in six hours, completing 3.7 feet a man hour in 1,176 man hours. The same company on the Ham-Noyon line laid 13,880 feet with 48 of their men and 411 unskilled labour in four hours, completing 7.5 feet a man hour in 1,836 man hours. "C" Company on the Omiecourt-Voyennes line laid 12,990 feet with 110 of their men and 372 unskilled labour in seven hours, completing 3.8 feet a man hour in 3,374 man hours. On the Pithon Wood Loop, "D" Company laid 6,300 feet of steel in 6½ hours with 60 of their own men and 120 labourers, completing 5.4 feet a man hour in 1,170 man hours. Total steel laid was 9.8 miles. The figure for "A" Company was high as their material was offloaded at convenient points from the Canal along the grade, but "B" and "C" were handicapped by lack of material or tractor power. The average footage a man hour was 6.9 feet.

On the Brie-Fay line at the Somme crossing fill, the work of hauling material for the Brie "Y" cut was continued, and at the Fay end 3,000 feet of grading was accomplished. The steel party of "B" Company with carrying parties of the 86th Labour Company laid 5,596 feet of track. The work of laying was nearly interrupted several times before noon as the supply of spikes ran low, but Lieut. Boon salvaged enough to keep the parties going. At 3 p.m. the supply of fish plates was exhausted, so steel laying had to cease. Decking and trimming the east bridge over the Somme was completed and 800 feet of steel laid and ballasted between the east and west bridges. As the next day was St. Patrick's Day the 10th Royal Irish Rifles party attending Divine service in an orchard near Cugny wore shamrock. An air of precaution permeated the area near the camp and all around, and defence trenches were being built with wire. Rumours of the forthcoming offensive were persistent, but there was no definite information. The next day "A" Company, in addition to other tasks, laid 2,000 feet of steel on the Chauny-Noyon line, "B" on the Brie-Fay line 5,200 feet, while "C" laid out the Fouchette Yard on the Omiecourt-Nesle-Voyennes line. Capt. J. T .Wright, C.A.M.C., arrived the following day to relieve Lieut. Button as medical officer.

The Battalion thus continued steadily with the work on all lines, but there were only a few hours left before the deluge. The enemy was now on the eve of his gigantic throw for victory, having realized that if he did not break the Allied line now he never would. The fates for him looked propitious, for Russia and its millions were out of the war, and he had thus been able to concentrate most of his resources on the Western Front.

CHAPTER IX

MARCH, 1918: THE GERMAN BID FOR VICTORY

The troops in the Fifth Army area were ordered to stand to at 5 a.m. on 20th March, 1918, and all day guns were moving forward. On going to IIIrd Corps at 9 a.m., Major Holdsworth discovered that the order to stand to did not apply to the 2nd Battalion, Canadian Railway Troops, but the unit was assured that orders would be sent if any more were necessary. The Battalion, therefore, continued with its work on all lines that day, but at 4.30 the next morning, the 21st, a most intense bombardment began along the entire front, the drum fire continuing without the slightest intermission until after 11.30 a.m., when the mist, previously thick as pea soup, thinned a little. About 2 p.m. artillery limbers began passing Battalion Headquarters retiring, their arrival so exciting the Italian labour nearby that they left camp immediately, strewing their kit along as they withdrew. The Chinese labour also made good time in retiring. With the Artillery came reports that the enemy attack was driving the troops back, while he had used a great deal of gas against the British Infantry and Artillery.

At 4 p.m. Brig.-Gen. J. Stewart of Headquarters, Canadian Railway Troops, visited the unit, and an hour later Col. Clarke issued orders to load the heavy stores and pack the remainder in readiness for a move, by which time shrapnel was dropping along the Flavy-Le Martel-Ham road. "C" Company was ordered to withdraw its advanced maintenance parties to Flavy and thence to the Headquarters Camp at Cugny. In the evening Col. Clarke and Major Gibson visited the Assistant Director of Light Railways at Bussy, but he had little information, merely saying he wished the work on the Voyennes line rushed and the Ham-Pithon Wood loop completed to allow the evacuation of rolling stock from the Flavy lines. A despatch rider was sent to the IIIrd Corps to bring the unit word of a move, as the guns were falling back and a move looked inevitable. The heavy mist had again descended. Col. Clarke issued instructions to "B" Company to place every effort on building the three lines from Ham: to Voyennes, to Noyon and to Pithon Wood.

While the unit had no definite information as to the situation as to the immense enemy offensive, "A" Company was ordered to stand to in the event of emergency, as all other units in the area were doing, while general maintenance was carried on as usual by the detached posts. The Rond d'Orleans line in front of Pierremande came under heavy shell fire and was broken by traffic, so one break was repaired to carry trains to the farthest point to which traffic was running. Chauny and Abbecourt Yard were heavily shelled at intervals throughout the day, but Cpl. Banks and a party of "A" Company men and some of the 84th Labour Company continued loading material at the latter place. Although the party had several narrow escapes, fortunately no casualties occurred. Work on the Somme crossing was carried on as usual by 25 of the Italian labour with the detail of "B" Company left under Lieut. McPherson. A motor lorry load of company stores accompanied by Lieut. Bonn was moved to the new Company Headquarters at Guiscard. Major Adams went to Battalion Headquarters with eight men for transfer to the 1st Battalion, Canadian Railway Troops, about to go to Egypt. Considering the improbability of receiving transport under the circumstances, he also arranged to ship more stores early the next morning, and send the men by train.

That morning (the 21st) Major Craig visited the three maintenance parties of "C" Company at Montescourt-Lizerolles, Frières-Faillouel and at Villequier-Aumont. At 1.30 p.m., Lieut. Cameron, with the first party, rang Company Headquarters to advise that as the Light Railway Operating crews had left the work, it would be wise to withdraw the parties to Flavy-LeMartel. Early in the afternoon, Major Craig visited the other three platoons at Mesnil-St. Nicaise and on his return to Flavy found that a move was imperative, so four waggons were loaded and the party there moved to Cugny, leaving only a small guard over the stores. The other parties at Frières-Faillouel and Villequier-Aumont were ordered to retire to the rendezvous, 7 Rue de Nesle, Guiscard. Soon after the opening of the enemy bombardment the same morning, the enemy began to shell the Foreste Railhead, succeeding in blowing the grade in four places, but these were repaired. Parties of "D" Company were sent to repair breaks reported at Pithon, Ham and at Ville-

Scholles, where the party succeeded in getting out a train load of ammunition. The enemy shelled the whole Foreste area thoroughly, using many gas shells and steadily advancing. By the afternoon the front line units were retiring through the village, so "D" Company packed all equipment ready to move at once. During the night the Abbecourt neighbourhood was heavily bombed by the enemy.

The despatch rider returned from IIIrd Corps with orders to move at 4.15 a.m. on the 22nd, so reveille was blown five minutes later on a very misty morning. At 8 a.m. the already loaded transport, the remaining important stores of records and the tools left Battalion Headquarters, Cugny, for Guiscard, a party of 30 of the Headquarters detail being left behind with Major Holdsworth and Lieut. Muir. Five waggons and a lorry returning at noon took as much of the important stores as they could, part of the huts and some 15 grade scrapers being left. Before Major Holdsworth and Lieut. Muir left at 6 p.m., Maurepas Farm was full of 9.2-inch guns and the field pieces had moved back west of Flavy. Large numbers of enemy aircraft flew over and shot up the roads and masses of troops with machine guns. In the morning Col. Clarke visited "D" Company at Foreste and with Major Gibson later went to the crossing under construction over the Ham road to allow rolling stock to be moved to the Voyennes line. This work had to be done by a party from "B" Company, as the 90th Labour Company had been ordered to move back to Roye by their Director. Considerable rolling stock was removed, but as usual one of the locomotives ran out of water and in going forward for more ran off the road, stopping all further work. Numerous enemy high velocity shells made the work very hazardous.

Ham was evacuated by the civilians by noon, and the sight of the refugees with their few treasured belongings in small carts was pitiful. The town was, moreover, full of "retiring" Italian and Chinese labour. By midnight Headquarters details and "B"Company were settled at Guiscard. The party of "C" Company at Flavy stayed at Mesnil-St. Nicaise. One "A" Company steel party with some of the 84th Labour Company laid 2,000 feet of steel towards Noyon, while Lieut. Macdonald continued ballasting on that line and Lieut. Draper and his platoon loaded material and did general maintenance in Abbecourt Yard. Lieut. Ritchie stood to in camp waiting for a truck to transport the survey party, but this did not arrive. Lieut. W. R. Smith visited the outposts in charge of Cpls. Fawn and Duggan, and went over the Rond d'Orleans line as far as the Kingston control to find the line broken in 16 places. The materials for repair were collected and the work was just started when the 84th Labour Company party got orders to move at once to Noyon. Because of heavy shelling the 2nd C.R.T. party had to be withdrawn temporarily from the work, and before it was able to continue, the Operating Company abandoned the idea of operating the line, so there was no point in attempting further repairs.

At Abbecourt, Capt. Ternan visited the various outposts and parties that day and in the evening went to Battalion Headquarters for information and orders. At 6 p.m. all traffic on the line in advance of Abbecourt was discontinued, so the detached posts were ordered back to camp. Abbecourt Yard and the vicinity of the Camp were shelled all day. At 11 p.m. the 54th Light Railway Operating Company, R.E., received orders from the Assistant Director of Light Railways to move all rolling stock down the canal line towards Noyon, thus blocking the line by which "A" Company hauled all material from Abbecourt Yard to continue laying steel towards Noyon. Fortunately "A" had already placed three cars of steel at the end of the line ready for the following day's work, and there happened to be ten cars of ties near the end of steel, which the company was able to carry forward. Chauny was evacuated that day. At 7.30 a.m., a motor lorry laden with tools, stores and kit of "B" Company set off from Le Mesnil for Guiscard, while Major Adams, Lieut. Bonn and a party went to Ham to continue the work there. Lieut. McPherson and a small party of "B" Company continued with the task on the Somme crossing to clear the rolling stock, and the remaining 80 men of the company were left in Le Mesnil. Major Adams left word that Sgt. Tack was to take 69 of these and report to Ham by lorry if possible, while the other 11 remained at Le Mesnil under C.S.M. Armstrong to clear the camp. As Sgt. Tack's parties had not reached Ham by 11 p.m., Major Adams at midnight found them on the station platform at Nesle. After some trouble, he made arrangements with the French to provide a train to take the party to Ham at 5 a.m. the next morning.

That day a lorry was sent to Flavy-le Martel to take the remaining stores to Mesnil-St. Nicaise, and another took the party at Cugny to the same town. On returning to Flavy for stores which had been left there, it was found that the old Company Headquarters had practically been destroyed by shell fire. At Foreste firing continued all the night of the 21st/22nd, so Capt. Galbraith hearing that the enemy were not far distant and still advancing, decided to retire "D" Company to Voyennes, starting at 3 p.m. and leaving a small party for maintenance of the lines. The Company was billeted in Voyennes that night, and was joined at 8 p.m. by the rear party, who reported that they had been driven out by machine gun fire so heavy that part of the equipment had to be left. The roads were blocked with traffic, chiefly civilians, who impeded progress greatly with their animals and carts. Several men of other units accompanied "D" Company. All that evening enemy aircraft were overhead near Battalion Headquarters at Guiscard and dropping bombs in the surrounding country.

Leaving orders that Headquarters and those of "B" Company at Guiscard move that day to Roye, Col. Clarke early on the 23rd went to visit the Assistant Director Light Railways, Fifth Army, South, but a message was received from him at 10 a.m. cancelling this order and giving instructions instead to move to Lassigny at once. "B" Company and part of their stores left by lorry and waggons at 2.15 p.m., moving by way of Munrancourt, Bussy and Sermaize. On arrival back at Guiscard about 3 p.m., Col. Clarke said that the enemy was in Nesle and that no word had been received from "C" and "D" Companies. The remainder of the men except 30 who marched with Lieut. Muir, leaving at 6 p.m., arrived back at Guiscard about 9 p.m. and started back to Lassigny about midnight. The roads were filled with incoming French troops taking over part of the Fifth Army front. Late in the evening Col. Clarke learned that "C" and "D" Companies got away in safety, but were the last troops but the infantry to leave. Air activity was noticeable all evening. At Lassigny everyone slept in the open in the centre of the old system of trenches fought over by the French a year previously. As all other units had been evacuated from the vicinity of Abbecourt, and "A" Company's only work now was extending the line to Noyon, it was decided to move camp closer to the job, so one platoon was held in camp under Lieut. W. R. Smith for the move, which was carried out with three waggons to Abbecourt Bridge, where everything was loaded on light railway cars and in the evening these moved as far back as the track was clear; that is, opposite Babœuf. Ahead of that the line was blocked with 235 cars and 27 locomotives, more than half the cars being empty.

Lieut. McIlwraith that day continued work with the steel gang, laying 3,000 feet. At 3 p.m. Capt. Ternan with Lieuts. Ritchie, Draper and Macdonald and 45 other ranks of "A" Company took seven waggons and two tractors into Abbecourt Yard, and with three empty waggons found left there, loaded a mile and a half of track complete under shell fire and direct observation and hauled them to a point opposite Babœuf. All the Company's working parties that day were sent out with full equipment in the event of emergency. It was found impossible to move all equipment and such items as tent floors were left, but all of value was saved. Capt. Ternan arranged with Capt. Chedaine, the French officer in charge of canal transport, for a barge as the only way of getting steel forward. As the barge had not reported by 9 p.m., Lieut. W. R. Smith went to Pont l'Evêque and found that the British guard had refused to allow it to go up the canal past Noyon bridge. With him on board, the barge went up again and after some argument was permitted to proceed, reaching the Company bivouac opposite Babœuf at 1 a.m. Major Adams reached Guiscard at 2.15 a.m. that day (the 23rd) and about 3.30 a.m. Major Graham asked him to provide a relief at daylight, so at 6 a.m. Major Adams accompanied by Lieut. Bonn went to Ham to meet Sgt. Tack and his party, but found the enemy in to the north of the town, machine gun bullets spattering in the street and the atmosphere very misty, so decided to report back to Guiscard. Later he sent Lieut. Bonn to Nesle to try to find Sgt. Tack and his party and instruct them to report to Battalion Headquarters, but in the meantime orders came to evacuate Guiscard for Nesle, so just after lunch "B" Company loaded. As they were on the point of moving off, new orders came from Nesle informing them that conditions were serious and ordering a move southwest to Lassigny, where they arrived between 8 and 9 p.m., to sleep in the open. Lieut. Bonn arrived later, reporting that he had seen Sprs. Evers, Slack and Taylor near Roye and ordered them to go towards Amiens.

All the working parties of "C" Company which could be placed on the Omiecourt-Voyennes line were employed in laying 3,000 feet of steel that day. Hearing that the enemy was steadily advancing by night marches, the Officer Commanding "D" Company at Voyennes again decided to move at 2 a.m., Lieut. Wills being detailed to find billets at the next village. Under command of Capt. Galbraith, with Lieuts. Knox and Sharp following, the company reached Languevoisin at 5 a.m. At 2 p.m. the company marched again to Rethonvillers, the men behaving splendidly under the trying circumstances encountered. As the people of the villages *en route* left a good deal of farm stock, the Company had no difficulty throughout the retirement in getting good meals, as the men made full use of everything so that it should not fall into the hands of the enemy, following closely behind.

At noon on the 24th the men of the Headquarters details marched to a French military hutment three-quarters of a mile from Lassigny, the Battalion transport remaining at the first camp site. All day and night troops were retiring through Lassigny, and Battalion stood ready to move on the receipt of any order. At Babœuf "A" Company transshipped track material from the train to the barge beginning at daylight. Lieut. Ritchie and a party distributed steel from the barge, while Lieut. McIlwraith and another party cleared 3,200 feet, which took the track under the Noyon bridge, and placed two switches for a marshalling yard to hold rolling stock. With a party of 14 men, Lieuts. Draper and Macdonald went back to Quierzy to collect a load of ties, finding the travelling workshop in the siding there on the point of being blown up and abandoned by the Royal Engineers in charge. They arranged to attach the workshop to their tractors, which pulled the whole train back towards Noyon. The R. E. turned over the keys and left to find their own company. The 54th Light Railway Operating Company, R.E., abandoned a large part of their company stores and equipment and turned over the rolling stock to the South African Operating Company. The latter fired up the locomotives and moved the line of waggons about three-quarters of a mile over the newly-built track, so that the head of the line was at Noyon bridge.

Lieut. W. R. Smith moved camp again that day to that place, where the company planned to bivouac for the night and continue laying steel the next morning, but about 6 p.m. the South Africans got orders to remove injectors and magnetos, destroy all stores and withdraw. As this made further tracklaying useless, the Company was reluctantly forced to relinquish the idea of moving the rolling stock farther from the enemy. For the past three days the civilian population had been evacuating Noyon. The Company equipment and stores had been loaded on the barge that day, so they now moved down to Pont l'Evêque, where they bivouaced for the night. From that time on their moves were governed by those of the barge, which was ordered farther back by the French authorities when they considered it necessary. After breakfast that morning, "B" Company and Battalion Headquarters moved to a Camp Militaire, east of Lassigny Station, the Officers in tents and the men in huts. A few stragglers left on the previous day's move reported.

The civil population had left Mesnil-St. Nicaise during the night under orders from their own officials, and as the morning advanced the British Artillery opened fire on points behind the town. Later in the morning when Major Craig learned that the infantry was holding the road a mile west of the town, he saw that an immediate withdrawal of working parties and the retirement of "C" Company were necessary. The four or five waggons were brought back from the line and loaded with all valuable equipment and rations which could be carried, and at 12 noon half the company with full kit moved towards Guiscard by way of Nesle under Lieut. Cameron. The remainder left camp at 1.30 under Major Craig. During a short rest at Nesle, a despatch rider informed Major Craig that the Germans were close to the town, so the move went on, the party just clearing the town as it was being barricaded. Just past the southwestern outskirts of the town, Major Craig threw out a rearguard, and when information was received that Battalion Headquarters had moved from Guiscard to Lassigny, the route was altered and the Company billeted for the night in the Chateau at Beaulieu-La Fontaine, remaining there that day in accordance with instructions from Col. Clarke, practising rearguard manoeuvres. Towards midnight orders came to go to the Battalion rendezvous at Ansauvillers. At 4 p.m. "D" Company under Capt. Galbraith marched to Lancourt, where the men were billeted for the night.

Following the transport which had left with as much of the essential stores as possible, Headquarters details left Lassigny on foot at 10.30 a.m. on the 25th for Tricot under Major Gibson by way of Marieul-la Mort to Ressons, where they were met by the lorries returning from Tricot after offloading. The transport parked in a field at Tricot near a French hospital, the town being full of refugees. The French guns were moving forward all evening, their transport of guns and supplies being first class. At 7.30 a.m. "A" Company's barge was ordered down the canal, this time going as far as Thourotte, where an empty building was found for the whole company. Capt. Ternan went to Battalion Headquarters, returning with Major Holdsworth. Col. Clarke also met the Company on its way down the canal bank and said it would be moved from Thourotte to join the rest of the Battalion. "B" Company marched to Ressons-sous-Metz, where lorries conveyed it to Tricot. At 12.30 a.m. "C" Company left Beaulieu-La Fontaine, reaching Popincourt at 5.30 a.m. and bivouacing until noon, moving off for Montdidier, where the British Commandant refused the Company billets for the night, but the French gave them accommodation in Adrian huts. "B" Company reached Couchy-les Potts at 2 a.m. on the 26th and halted for the night, after experiencing much difficulty on the march from traffic and refugees.

Headquarters remained at Tricot on the 26th, which "D" Company reached shortly after noon. Near Roye that day, Capt. Draper, the Quartermaster, reported that the town was being shelled. Reports were received that some of the men who had become detached from their companies had been put into the line. Sgt. Vincent, who left Cugny for "D" Company at Foreste on the 22nd, was believed to be a prisoner or a casualty, as no more word had been heard of him. At 3.30 p.m. at Thourotte, "A" Company was ordered by the Commandant du Service de la Navigation to move its barge farther back, which necessitated the Company moving with it. When it reached the locks at Longue, the French Engineers were hurriedly evacuating valuable timber and supplies of steel with few men to do the work. "A" Company, therefore, volunteered their services, which were accepted at once, with the result that 20,000 feet of timber was formed into a boom ready for towing down the Canal, and 50 tons of steel rails and interlocking steel sheet piling was loaded on barges, with four tons of flour and the records of the Navigation Company, besides large quantities of civilian property. The civilians left at Longueil were anxious to get away immediately, so at Capt. Chedaine's request, "A" Company helped expedite the evacuation.

A few refugees on the road from other villages very short of food were helped by the men of "A" Company, who shared their biscuits and bully beef with them. On several occasions the men were able to feed needy civilians as they passed the field kitchens, their appreciation and profuse expressions of gratitude amply repaying the men for a little shortage in their own rations. The Company left on the last barge about 6 p.m., disembarking at the locks at Compiegne and marching a mile farther down the Canal bank to bivouac for the night. One officer remained with the barge, which was delayed by the congestion of barges at the locks, and before he left the town it received a heavy bombing from enemy aircraft, bombs falling close to the barge on all sides. A large fire started close to the bivouac, and at the same time more aircraft bombed the adjacent area, the bivouac being showered by splinters, Cpl. G. V. Podger being seriously wounded in the head.

Early that day 30 other ranks of Lieuts. McPherson's and Tack's party of "B" Company reported to Tricot, having come with "D" Company from Roye. They reported that on the 23rd while trying to gain touch with Major Adams, they had been taken as stragglers by Military Police. Part had been sent up the line, but they themselves had later been allowed to start for the Battalion, as they had learned its location. At 2.30 p.m. "C" Company left Montdidier for Ansauvillers, where the Battalion was to assemble. "D" Company left Couchy-les Potts at 10.30 a.m. and finally reached Tricot at 3 p.m. Word came through that Sgt. Bowner of "D" Company had received a commission as lieutenant. Battalion Headquarters and "B" and "D" Companies left Tricot at 9.45 a.m. on the 27th for the rendezvous at Ansauvillers, to which the transport and "C" Company had already gone. "A" Company was still in the south and part of "B" was still to arrive. New instructions, however, perhaps not entirely unexpectedly, altered the role of the Battalion suddenly, and for a time it reverted to its original status as infantry.

CHAPTER X

IN THE LINE AS INFANTRY

After the close of February, 1918, the Eastern front disappeared, enabling Germany to bring enough troops to the West to render impotent the small Allied superiority in numbers they previously possessed. The result was that in March the opposing fronts were about equal in numbers, but the enemy could quickly call up more reinforcements, which would add to her numbers 250,000 men. While the American forces were steadily increasing, it would still be several months before they would be a strong factor in the field. It was impossible for France to make any new effort, while there was not yet any recruitment in Britain large enough to fill the gaps made by Third Ypres and Cambrai. It would, therefore, be necessary for the Allies to fight defensively.

Ludendorff's object was to secure a decision in the western theatre inside four months by isolating the British Army, rolling it up from the right and pinning it to an entrenched camp between the Somme and the Channel, and holding it with few troops; sweeping on the French, and putting them out of the fight. He planned, therefore, to thrust with all the strength he could muster at the point of junction of Haig and Pétain. To effect this object, the Germans had withdrawn six divisions from Italy and several from the Balkans; they had half of the 1920 class of recruits ready, and had also transferred almost 500,000 men from the East. Including captures from Italy and Russia and those transferred from the East, Ludendorff had a tremendous concentration of guns, while the network of French railways within his front enabled him to achieve a local superiority, and to concentrate swiftly where he wished to strike, his dispositions enabling him to threaten the French in Champagne and the British at St. Quentin. He would thus divide the Allied forces, hem in the British and smash the French, and to do this would break the British right centre.

The enemy now had 192 divisions in the West, more than half concentrated against the British, the actual front of attack being from Croisilles on the Sensée to Vendeuil on the Oise, a span of more than 50 miles, and Ludendorff planned to use 37 divisions, or more than 500,000 men, as his first assault force, to be followed by new troops in a wheel without end. This plan envisaged driving the British behind the upper Somme by the close of the first day, and so on the next force a general withdrawal of the entire line, while on the following day he would launch a great attack on the British front at Arras. Success in that quarter would result in total disaster to the British right wing and a withdrawal towards Amiens and the Channel. He would then turn on Pétain.

New German tactical methods were to be employed, based chiefly on the highly specialized training of various units, and involving local superiority. The old German conception of massing troops near the front of attack was to be avoided, troops being brought up by night marches just prior to zero hour. There was also an absence of a lengthy artillery preparation, the assault being preceded by a bombardment of brevity and intensity, while the rear areas of the enemy would be laid under a deluge of gas shells. In small groups, selected troops carrying light trench mortars and many machine guns would assault, supported by field batteries. This method of infiltration would open a breach, through which following troops would penetrate, dislocating the opposing front until it crumbled. The German superiority in numbers would enable him to advance far past the protected areas and at least far enough to take the enemy's artillery positions.

While the Allies knew that the attack impended, the enemy concentration in the angle of the immense salient rendered it impossible for them to decide until the last moment where it would strike, particularly as other areas were also threatened. The right wing of the British was held by Sir Hubert Gough's Fifth Army* in front of St. Quentin, and late in January its front had been extended to the right as far

---

* Eleven divisions: 9th, 21st, 16th, 66th, 24th, 61st, 30th, 36th, 14th, 18th, and 58th, in that order, with the 39th, 50th and 20th in reverse and the 1st and 2nd Cavalry Divisions.

south as Barisis on the left bank of the Oise, so the Fifth Army now held a line of 72,000 yards, or more than 41 miles. On the left was Sir Julian Byng's Third Army of four corps just north of the Arras-Douai road to the vicinity of Gouzeaucourt in the south.

To make up for its weakness in numbers, the British force built defences of great strength, in front a forward zone of two sectors: a line of outposts to give the alarm and withdraw, and a strongly-wired line of resistance, in which were well-sited redoubts 2,000 yards apart, with the intervals covered by a barrage of field and heavy guns. The line of resistance and the redoubts were to be held to the end. In rear of the forward zone was the battle zone on a similar plan, but for the absence of outposts. A defence in depth, it was strongly wired and defended by redoubts and other strong points. In rear of it a mile or so away was the last defensive zone, less well protected and when the battle began still incomplete. Although no strong alternative positions had been prepared in rear because of the few men available, a strong bridgehead position was in course of preparation to cover Péronne and the Somme crossings to the south.

At 4.45 a.m. on 21st March, the fire of the entire weight of the enemy's immense mass of guns was let loose against the British forward and battle zones, headquarters, lines of communication and artillery positions, while the rearward areas were drenched in gas which clung close in the fog. Also under fire were the French sectors north and northeast of Rheims, north of Arras and in the La Bassée-Lys line, while Messines and the Ypres area were heavily attacked and Dunkirk was bombarded from the sea. While the batteries of the Third and Fifth Armies replied, the visibility had closed to 50 yards, the only means of communication being by wireless, which then was slow and not entirely trustworthy. Through the mist groups of the enemy at all points filtered forward to cut wire and penetrate the outpost positions.

At varying times the enemy infantry advanced, and it was not long before the troops in the outpost line under the artillery bombardment and the gas were in a desperate position. Soon the outposts had gone and the enemy was fighting in the forward zone, which put up a stout resistance until late in the day. When the fog lifted about one o'clock, enemy aircraft flying low attacked troops and gun positions with machine guns. Before 11 a.m. arrived news at headquarters that the Germans were through the forward zone on the far right opposite La Fère, and the same north of the Bapaume-Cambrai road and at Lagnicourt and Bullecourt. At noon the enemy was in Ronssay in the battle zone itself; were in contact with the rear defences of the battle zone, and threatened to break through down the valley of the Omignon. Elsewhere they were still held, but it was serious that by noon they had reached the battle zone and at Ronssay penetrated it.

By nightfall against 19 British divisions in line the enemy had hurled 37 as a first move and before dark 64 in all were in action. The greatest aggregate German advance was about 8,000 yards on the extreme right, while the Fifth Army was outnumbered four to one and the main enemy effort was against that Army. By the afternoon of the 22nd the whole of the Fifth Army was in the third defensive position, but the Third Army had managed to surrender little ground. On the Fifth Army front, however, south of Orignon the enemy smashed through a gap and broke the third zone around Vaux and Beauvois. At 11 p.m. Gough ordered a withdrawal to the bridgehead position east of the Somme, as yet incomplete, while the Third Army was forced to retire to conform. As his right flank was in peril, and had fallen back to a weak position, without hope of securing fresh troops in the face of an enemy hourly becoming stronger, early on the 23rd Gough instructed one Corps to withdraw to the river line and another to a position between Doingt and Nurlu, the latter just covering Péronne. In the face of unceasing attacks this was done. That evening the enemy announced that the first stage of the immense battle had closed. He had advanced at the deepest point some nine miles.

On the 24th the enemy widened the breach between the two Armies at the bend of the Somme, so the right and centre of the Third Army again withdrew in the face of the deep, broad wedge the Germans had driven into the centre of the British front. Continued pressure on the 25th compelled the further retirement of the front east of Noyon before dark, but the French now appeared in enough strength to send one corps to help the Fifth Army. The next day it was announced that Foch was assuming the supreme command of the Allied forces in the West.

On the 25th Gough began to assemble an assorted special force consisting of stragglers, details returning to units, the personnel of a machine gun school, army troops, tunnelling companies and American and Canadian engineers, including the 2nd Canadian Railway Troops. On the 26th under the command of Maj.-Gen. Grant, chief engineer of the Fifth Army, they prepared the old line of the Amiens defences from Mezières by Marcelcave to the Somme at Hamel, and later Brig.-Gen. Sandeman Carey, a field artillery officer returning from leave, was placed in charge to command the detachment throughout the subsequent operations. This force was the only reserve available for this very vital sector, orders having been given to withdraw to the position Le Quesnoy-Rosières-Proyart and to link with the Third Army at Bray.

On his arrival at Ansauvillers at 1.30 p.m. on the 27th, Col. Clarke at once called a conference of all officers in "C" Company Headquarters, announcing that he had had a visit from a Staff Officer of Fifth Army, who gave him an order to report the Battalion to General Carey, commanding the Amiens defences at Villers-Bretonneux and that all arrangements had already been made to embus at 5.30 p.m. at the crossroads west of Wavignies. General Carey was informed that the unit would arrive at 9 p.m. in 20 busses 400 strong to be put in his line as far north as the road to Fouilloy. The 2nd C.R.T. was then organized into a transport branch to be moved to a more convenient point to Villers-Bretonneux, and the main body, which had to be hurriedly equipped for emergency. All the Staff Officer could tell Col. Clarke at the time was that he believed the unit was to be used for construction work, "but he was so indefinite that no reliance could be placed on it." All going forward were equipped with rifle, respirator, steel helmet, at least 50 rounds of ammunition and two days rations. The transport was ordered to go to Sains-en-Amienois, whence it could maintain touch with the unit.

At 5.30 p.m. the officers of the Battalion and 380 other ranks formed up in the village square under Major Gibson, Col. Clarke and Major Holdsworth leaving by car to interview General Carey and secure information as to the unit's movements. The Battalion embussed, moving by Breteuil, Moreuil and Boves to the junction of the main Amiens-Vermand road south of Blagny-le-Tronville, and thence directly to Villers-Bretonneux. As the convoy had been on continuous duty since the 21st, the trip was punctuated with breakdowns, which finally caused it to be divided into three sections, the first arriving at 11.30 p.m., the second an hour later, and the third at 8 a.m. Each section was unceremoniously dumped at the extreme western end of the town without any sign of the guide, as had been arranged, so the men of the first section were placed in the lee of buildings out of the wind and made as comfortable as possible, while the officers began a search for a Headquarters. At a Brigade Headquarters, they were informed they were to take over a portion of the line before daylight. It seemed hardly credible that men without any recent training would be put into the line without warning, but the party prepared to make the best of it. A Staff Captain who had promised to meet the unit and supply the stores it needed failed to turn up, so the party set out to find stores around the town. They met a Canadian Officer attached to a British Ordnance unit, who turned over everything he had in his store, including 16 machine guns and two lorry loads of ammunition.

As the third section carrying "D" Company, Headquarters and all but one platoon of the men had not arrived by 2 a.m., it was decided to leave the platoon under Lieut. Knox which had arrived to join the Company to guide it to an arranged rendezvous. The remainder moved off towards Warfusée-Abancourt. At a certain point guides were to meet the party to direct it to the unit's positions. When the Battalion had marched a way down the main road, an officer rode up, introduced himself and announced he would guide it to Brigade Headquarters, so the unit sheltered in an aerodrome nearby while Major Gibson accompanied the officer. At Brigade Headquarters, he met Col. Clarke and Major Holdsworth, who had already made a tour of the lines the unit was to occupy. In their retirement, the 61st Division on the right and the 39th Division on the left had left a gap between them. Discovering this, an enemy patrol with machine guns had got through and occupied the eastern end of Warfusée-Abancourt. Carey's force, including the 2nd C.R.T., was to be thrown in to stem this breach, but more than this little was known of the situation.

A guide was furnished Major Gibson to direct him with the Battalion to an officer in the line who was to allot the unit its position. At the aerodrome where the unit had been left, a Staff Captain from Brigade Headquarters arrived, claiming to be the official guide and desiring to take the unit to an entirely different position. When it was pointed out that the instructions conflicted, a discussion took place between the two guides, resulting in the Staff Officer returning to Brigade Headquarters for more instructions. There he remained, but another Staff Captain arriving claimed to know the unit's exact position in the line. He led the Battalion along the Marcelcave road to a railway crossing, where he turned back on the Warfusée-Abancourt road and halted, interviewing an officer in charge of that part of the line. The latter told him he had made his dispositions for the night and did not feel like getting out of bed to change them, but suggested that the Battalion stay where it was until morning, when he would indicate a location. As the place in which he suggested the unit rest was an open field swept by a raw north wind, the officers refused to leave their men in the open and marched them back to a wood, where shelter was found in some tents and gunpits. Here the unit assumed a position in general reserve at 4.30 a.m., when all the men not needed as picquets rolled into their blankets.

After an hour's rest, the men were aroused and set digging short sections of trench in the wood and establishing Lewis gun positions. At Brigade Headquarters the unit was informed that a counter-attack was to be made at 5 a.m. on Warfusée-Abancourt by the 61st Division, but this did not take place until 10 a.m. and within an hour petered out entirely, partly owing to the British wire and also to the fact that the enemy had moved forward in the night to the west end of the town and had located machine guns in buildings and in a cemetery there, while the Division's barrage had been directed almost entirely to the eastern end.

Immediately after the failure of this attack, the position of the 2nd C.R.T. in the wood came under an intense bombardment, and as the unit was now part of the front line system, since the original line of defence on its immediate front had dissolved with the collapse of the 61st Division, it became evident at once that the Battalion's position was untenable, while being held in its original formation as a reserve, owing to too many men massed. The unit at once established Lewis guns in the position already dug in the cemetery and through the wood and then withdrew "B" and "C" Companies to positions astride the railway. Despite considerable shell fire, this movement was made in good order, and on reaching the new positions the men began digging with tools salvaged in the morning. Just prior to this movement, "D" Company under Capt. Galbraith, delayed by the non-arrival of their Section of the convoy until 8 a.m., arrived and at once went into position south of the railway and 800 yards in front of Marcelcave, to dig trenches. The unit was thus prepared to meet the threatened enemy attack in an excellent position, rising ground back of its support and reserve trenches giving a good field of fire in the event of attack. By 3 p.m. all troops occupying the forward trenches had cleared the Battalion front and taken positions in its rear and on its flanks.

In the meantime the enemy appeared uncertain whether to consolidate his position in Marcelcave or push his forces forward. The Battalion reserved its fire all afternoon, first to give the enemy an opportunity of showing his hand, and secondly to prevent his securing too intimate a knowledge of the unit's Lewis guns until he began an attack. Later in the afternoon, he attacked north of the Amiens road, but it did not spread as far as the Battalion's lines. Towards evening rain began to fall, and as it continued all night it added greatly to the discomfort of the men in the trenches. That night and in the early morning two patrols were sent out, one under Capt. Galbraith and the other under Lieut. Knox to determine the enemy's position. They found him treating the village of Marcelcave with respect, and that place unoccupied except by scattered machine gun posts. The trenches to the left of the 2nd C.R.T. were occupied by the Bedford Yeomanry, while on the right a battalion of the Gloucesters held the line with numerous stragglers in support and reserve.

In the meantime on the Oise Canal south of Compiegne, the French had the canal sufficiently clear to allow "A" Company to get more material ready for evacuation. The company boomed 50,000 feet of big bridge timbers near the Compiegne locks and then moved about three kilometres up the canal and boomed 320 telegraph poles, each about 25 feet long. At 1.45 p.m., the company received orders to prepare for a move by bus to Sains-en-Amienois, but the busses failed to arrive. At Ansauvillers, as the mechanical transport had not returned by 11 a.m. and the French Cavalry had retired through the town for Montdidier, Lieut. Muir sent 30 other ranks in charge of Capt. Allan, the unit Chaplain, to march to Sains. Four lorries arriving at 1 p.m. were loaded with the remainder of the stores. The party with Capt. Allan was picked up *en route*, and all arrived at Sains-en-Amienois, where the animal transport had already been located.

In the Amiens defence line on the 29th after a night of rain until 1 p.m. the morning was grey and misty and the Battalion improved its positions. The day passed quietly, except for some sniping on all the positions by field and machine guns, which inflicted few casualties. The enemy's activities seemed to be directed to feeling out the positions of the troops on the right flank of the Battalion and in moving in and out of Marcelcave. In mid-morning he became more venturesome and at points began to dig machine gun positions. The Battalion then adopted an aggressive policy, continuing it all day, putting a stop to all work; confusing and worrying all traffic on the Warfusée-Abancourt-Marcelcave road and making any movement in its sector very difficult. At the same time the unit inflicted enough damage on the enemy to teach him respect. In the night two patrols sent out again under the same officers advanced to a depth of 1,000 yards, Capt. Galbraith's patrol encountering an enemy patrol, which it dispersed. Except for intermittent machine gun fire from the right, the night passed quietly.

In the night the Battalion was informed that an attack was to be made on the morning of the 30th by the troops on its right flank, but at dawn the unit's whole position, as well as the trenches on its right flank, came under a heavy bombardment by shell and machine gun fire, which increased in intensity as the morning advanced. Shortly after the bombardment started, the troops on the extreme right holding the ridge south of Marcelcave, began to retire, as far as the Battalion could see, to the south. At 11 a.m. the troops holding the front line trenches on the right flank of "D" Company also withdrew, leaving the right of "D" in the air. Large numbers of these troops crossed to the north of the railway, passing through the lines of "C" Company, spreading wild rumours and causing much uneasiness among the men. Then the troops on the immediate left of the Battalion began to go back, so as the Battalion was in danger of being cut off, the front line was ordered to retire on its support trenches, where each company was reorganized, reinforced by stragglers and prepared to advance to the unit's forward positions again, as the gap in the left was being filled. Capt. Galbraith with his machine guns first went forward, and covered by these the men again took up their former positions. In this advance Lieut. Knox was killed.

In the afternoon, the enemy advanced from the rear of Marcelcave to attack the unit's right flank, and as this led him along the slope of the hill in full view of the Battalion's trenches to the south of the railway, every advantage was taken by the 2nd C.R.T. Lewis gunners of the targets presented by his massed forces, and excellent results were obtained. Shelling and machine gun fire continued until night fell, but no more attacks were launched on this part of the line. In the evening the unit was ordered to supply a wiring party for its left flank, a party chiefly from "C" Company, except the Lewis gunners, and in charge of Major Gibson with all the men who had served as instructors in building wire entanglements in the unit's training in England. The party went to the cemetery, but found that the work had been cancelled, as units were to be relieved that night by the Anzacs, so returned to Villers-Bretonneux to billets. During the night the enemy showed great nervousness, keeping flares constantly in the air, a feeling aggravated by the Battalion's Lewis guns and rifles.

At 4.30 a.m. on the 31st, Easter Sunday, the Battalion was relieved by orders received from the 184th Brigade [1], and proceeded to Villers-Bretonneux, where it was met by lorries from the Battalion transport at Sains-en-Amienois, at which half the unit arrived at noon, when the transport returned for the remainder. The following officers and other ranks were mentioned for their example and for acts of courage under fire: Capt. R. D. Galbraith, Lieut. A. J. Bonn, Sgt. W. May, Cpls. (L/Sgts.) E. G. Saigle and S. Hill, Cpls. R. J. Killan and J. L. Glover, and Sprs. F. Daley, W. G. Douglas, F. S. Smith, M. De Lucia and J. L. C. Bogart. Although the unit had been in the line for 72 hours, it had only had 29 casualties, including two killed. That day "A" Company again began working with the French Engineers with two strong parties, one loading steel rails and steel sheet piling at Longueil docks, where the party salvaged about 500 hardwood ties and 50 tons of steel material. The second party made up another boom of telegraph poles.

Headquarters and "B", "C" and "D" Companies paraded in the orchard in rear of the Chateau at Sains-en-Amienois at 1 p.m. on 1st April in hollow squares, and after an inspection by the Commanding Officer, Hon. Capt. Allan, the Chaplain, conducted the funeral service of Lieut. Knox, the unit marching to a French cemetery in the town for the interment. "D" Company furnished the armed escort and the bugler. Major Holdsworth went to Courcelles-Sous-Moyencourt to make final arrangements for billeting the battalion there the next day. It was learned that the field Headquarters, Canadian Railway Troops, (Maj.-Gen. J. Stewart) were at Bernaville. "A" Company was busy removing from the Oise Canal the booms of timber and telegraph poles, which were drawn out on skidways built near Jaux and piled on the river bank. The next day the Battalion, less "A" Company, moved to Courcelles-sous-Moyencourt, where the men were billeted throughout the town and the Officers in a large Chateau owned by Capt. the Marquis de Ranst,

---

[1] Included in this formation besides the 2nd Battalion, Canadian Railway Troops, were the 2nd/5th Gloucesters, 2nd/4th Oxford and Buckinghamshire Light Infantry, 184th Machine Gun Company, Essex Yeomanry and 2nd/4th Royal Berkshire Regiment.

St. Busson. While the unit began a course of training and lectures the following day, Major Holdsworth and Lieut. Muir went to Compiègne to arrange for the movement of "A" Company thence to Courcelles, while Lieut. Stack with eight lorries went to Criel to meet "A" Company. That company completed its work, removing the third boom from the river and loading the remainder of the telegraph poles above Compiègne into a barge, 500 being salvaged that day. Ordered to move by barge to Criel to meet the unit transport, it was found impossible to get a tug for towing until the next morning. Early on the 4th, all stores were loaded on the barge, the horse transport left, and the company moved by barge to Criel. Capt. Ternan and two officers and 59 other ranks remained to unload the barge, while the remainder of the company left for Courcelles.

The following day the machine gun section of "C" and "D" Companies fired on the ranges, and while the remainder of the unit continued its training programme, Major Adams set out to search the neighbouring collecting camps for "B" Company's missing men, finding a corporal and 11 men in Amiens. Lieut. MacPherson, C.S.M. Armstrong, with two other non-commissioned officers and 18 sappers, became detached on 22nd March. Part of the party bivouaced near the Brie-Fay line and began the next day to put the line near Fay in shape to clear the rolling stock. The unballasted condition of the track caused several locomotives to topple over near Barleux. Sgt. J. Scott's work was commendable, his energetic example heartening everyone. This was very noticeable while a crossing was being put over the standard gauge at Fay, when shell fire was very heavy. At 7.30 in the evening, as everyone was leaving that part of the country, it was decided to move to Estrées, the mule transport by road in charge of C.S.M. Armstrong and the remainder by rail, using a tractor and three small trucks. The latter finally reached Estrées by midnight after much trouble from derailments. Before they left Assevillers, a battery of 6-inch howitzers was in action there.

On arrival at Estrées it was found that the line was so badly congested with traffic that the tractor and trucks could not go through, and the old French line was also blocked by the standard gauge having cut into it. The stores were piled into waggons and everyone went to sleep where he could between batteries of 8 and 9.2-inch guns. At 8 a.m. on the 24th an artillery officer came along the road telling everyone to leave at once, so the party started; had breakfast at Foucaucourt and reaching Framerville at noon drew rations. The party reached a point a little west of Lihons, where camp was pitched. At 8.30 p.m. the sentry left to guard the stores was warned by transport galloping past that the enemy had broken through to Chaulnes. The men were wakened and the transport started off, the remainder following on foot. Before the transport had gone far an officer on horseback ordered them to cut the mules loose and leave the waggons. Fortunately his instructions were not carried out, as it later turned out that the whole stampede was the work of enemy spies dressed in British uniforms. The foot party managed to get transportation on lorries and reached Lamotte before midnight. There all was confusion, enemy bombs raining down and machine gun fire sweeping the streets. On learning that the report of the enemy's advance was false, the party started back towards the camp near Lihons.

Less transport, detached in the previous night's turmoil, the party arrived at its destination by 5.30 a.m. By that time the British 18-pounder batteries were in action nearby, but few shells were coming, although some bombs were close. Lieut. MacPherson set out on a bicycle to try to find the transport but could discover no trace of it, but did get more rations. He had heard that some of the men of the unit were in Villers-Bretonneux. In the evening a westward move took place, and by midnight the party reached the vicinity of Lamotte and found cover for the night. Everyone had just gone to sleep when a message was received to board the train and evacuate the town at once of all available standard gauge stock. The party reached Villers-Bretonneux at 6 a.m., and thence went to Amiens. By that evening, (the 26th) Lieut. MacPherson found some of the missing transport and men, so the strength of the party was 22 all ranks once more. The party moved from Amiens on the 27th, had lunch at St. Vast to the north-west and stopped for the night in a farm near Vignacourt, where tents and rations were secured from a party of the 12th C.R.T. There they remained all the next day, which was cold and wet, still with no word of the whereabouts of the Battalion, although Lieut. MacPherson spent the day seeking information. At noon Cpl. G. A. House of "C" Company, Spr. G. M. Hodgson of "B" and Dvr. Gnaedinger of the mechanical transport section joined the party, bringing the strength to 25 all ranks, and the next day Spr. Leitch of "C" Company joined. On 1st April the party began work with the 12th C.R.T., who were building a line of trenches and wire entanglements near Vignacourt, and to the party was attached 250 Indian labour. The strength of the detachment reached 27 on the 2nd with the arrival of Spr. H. L. Price. On the 6th it was learned that Major Holdsworth and some of "C" and "D" Companies had been seen passing through Vignacourt on motor trucks, and the next afternoon Major Adams, passing through with "A" and "B" Companies, got in touch with the party, which rejoined the Battalion at Villers-l'Hôpital on the 8th.

A word about the unit's losses of equipment in the recent operations might be of interest at this point. At the time of the German push, the Battalion, it will be recalled, was operating on a front extending from near Peronne to Chauny, with a large number of maintenance parties well forward in the fighting area, while the remainder of the unit was building light railways near Noyon, Ham, Nesle, Foreste and Brie. Nearly all the tools and equipment with the maintenance parties were abandoned, as it was impossible to send transport to collect them. Similarly, the tools of the bridging party at Brie had to be left along with the work train, when the enemy passed the end of steel. The bulk of tools and equipment with the companies on construction was carried along with the transport, so the Battalion saved more than 60 per cent of its tools and 95 per cent of its surveying equipment, while all the heavy stores, machine shop and stock of wrought iron and steel were brought away on the stores train.

The Battalion moved on the 6th to Villers-l'Hôpital, where Battalion Headquarters was located in the Bureau de Ville. On the 8th Lieut. MacPherson's party of "B" Company rejoined, as has been recorded, as well as another party of "B" on leave since before 22nd March and held at the Base. Major Greenlees was transferred to the 13th C.R.T. Training continued in the new location, beginning with physical training, rifle exercises and musketry, with lectures and battalion parades and route marches, while the machine gun section and the band trained separately. Instruction in wire entanglements under Lieut. Ritchie, firing on the ranges and a sham battle followed, the companies participating in an attack manoeuvre. On the 11th 13 other ranks of "D" Company, missing since 22nd March, returned from various concentration camps. Word was also received that Spr. J. W. Schnurr, reported missing from 30th March, had been wounded acting as a stretcher bearer, and that Spr. A. Ross, missing since 23rd March, was in hospital in England. Orders came the next day to supply 300 others ranks to the 338th Roads Company, R.E., for repairing roads near Frohen-le Grand and Wavans for a few days. Ten other ranks (2) were awarded Military Medals for their good work while the Battalion was in the line. A day or two later word was received that Capt. Galbraith of "D" Company and Lieut. Bonn of "B" had each been awarded the Military Cross for gallant services in the same operations. Lieut. L. F. Johnston, the transport officer, was promoted temporary captain, dating from 11th February. Instructions arrived on the 16th for 400 other ranks to work at grading on a stone spur on standard gauge west of Wavans with scrapers. At noon on the 18th, half the transport with Headquarters and "A" and "B" Companies left for Frevant, (for the unit had been ordered to Calais) which they left by train for the coast, followed the next day by the remainder of the unit.

By 8th April the German offensive ended, the Allied front having been established and the road to Amiens closed, although the Germans held a position on the heights west of the Avre and on the plateau east of Villers-Bretonneux. For the time he had exhausted his strength in the Somme area and had increased the length of his front by 35 miles.

---

(2) Sgt. W. May and Cpl. (L/Sgt.) E. G. Saigle of "B" Company; Sprs. W. G. Douglas, M. DeLucia and R. J. Killan of "C", and Cpl. (A/Sgt.) S. Hill, Cpl. J. L. Glover and Sprs. J. L. C. Bogart, F. Daley and F. S. Smith of "D" Company.

CHAPTER XI

THE ST. OMER AREA

The first detachment of the 2nd C.R.T. was met at Vendroux Yards some three miles south of Calais on the afternoon of 19th April by a guide from the 298th Company, R.E., marching to camp a mile away. Clear of the terminal yards, the camp was fronted by a good road and a canal. Stores and the machine shop were placed in the Vendroux Yards. The remainder of the unit arrived early the following morning at Les Fontinettes Station, Calais, when "C" and "D" Companies marched to No. 6 West Leave Camp. It was arranged that "A" and "B" Companies begin work in the Vendroux Yards on the morrow to build about 17 miles of new sidings and ladder track there. The work represented a complicated piece of yard construction, as a double track running line cut the proposed yard diagonally and traffic had to be kept going while the work continued. Very early on the morning of the 21st, the enemy made an air raid on the Calais water front, but did not visit the area of the camp. In addition to the work in Vendroux Yards, the unit was asked to build a pile bridge over the Riviere Nieuve on the southwest side of the city, and for the purpose was given a Canadian pile driver. Another responsibility was a line to the sand dunes to eliminate the present system of hauling sand from the dunes through the numerous yards of Calais, necessitating many delays. It was strongly opposed by the French, so a short connection to the existing sand spur was not to be built until the connections to the Dunkirk branch were completed. As material could only come in on this line, however, it was necessary to insert a temporary connection. The unit was instructed to make this a "fake", so that no one could call it a railway.

Work on the sand dunes was begun on the 23rd by "C" and "D" Companies. Surveys were carried out the next day and information passed for French approval. "C" Company graded 900 feet on their sector of the line to the Dunkirk branch, while "A" and "B" Companies continued working in the Vendroux Yards. The unit undertook also to build a gun shop at Valdelièvre in the Ordnance Yard for the repair of broken parts the following day. Orders arrived on the 29th that the Battalion was to move to St. Momelin and Tilques, two towns to the north and west of St. Omer, so Col. Clarke and Capt. Draper left to report to the Assistant Director of Roads, Second Army, near St. Omer. Col. Clarke learned that the new camp would be at Tilques and Serques for the time being, but on the arrival of "C" and "D" by train at St. Omer at 1.15 p.m. the next day it was found that the French authorities had not been contacted, so the detachment was sent back to Watten by train. "A" and "B" Companies marched to Tilques, where they were billeted. "C" and "D" Companies were placed in billets at Serques by evening. Headquarters, Canadian Railway Troops, advised the unit that day that Col. Clarke had been awarded a bar to his D.S.O.

The unit now learned that its work was to be the construction of a road from Tilques across the low land to St. Momelin from south of Le Berstacke to Serques. The Tilques-St. Momelin road was to be built across country with 2 foot 6-inch fill, with a 6-inch layer of gravel, and topped by planks, while the other was to be made over the existing road, to be widened and gravel and planking placed where necessary. The plan was to provide extra roads to relieve the traffic east and west, and in the event of a retreat, permit flooding the low lands and still have a road system. This could be done in two days from inland and from the sea the first high tide, which meant two weeks at the most. At the present time the sea level was 12 feet higher than the land level in this area. On the afternoon of 1st May, Col. Clarke went over the proposed line with the Assistant Director of Roads, Second Army, while the survey parties of "A" and "B" Companies began work on the St. Momelin-Tilques road. Because a French division was moving into Tilques, "A" and "B" went under canvas that day, "A" Company in the grounds of a Chateau on the outskirts of the town, and "B" at St. Momelin. The unit was informed that it would receive as labour the 1st and 4th Middlesex Alien Labour Companies, units formed in England of aliens, who could not serve in the line. The next day "D" Company moved to Le Berstacke. On their section of the road following the old second class road southwestwards, the springy ground made planking necessary, while a great deal of brush would require clearing. "A" Company began grading the new road, while the survey party continued placing slope stakes and tieing in with the plan of work.

"B" Company started work that morning on the St. Momelin-Tilques road, and had to demolish a brick wall to begin grading. Arrangements were made at a conference between the Inland Water Transport, R.E., and a representative of the Bridge Department, G.H.Q., at which Major Gibson represented the Battalion the following day, for delivery of sleepers for planking by barges from Zenneghen to the bridge at Watten. Grading from St. Momelin was hampered by the low ground, the barrow pits filling with water after nine inches of earth was removed. Scrapers were used for a time, but the mules sank in the mud easily, but a thin layer could be removed and the remainder taken away by wheelbarrows. A draft of 38 other ranks from the C.R.T. Depot, Purfleet, nearly all Russians and to be kept on probation for a time, arrived on the 5th. Arrangements were made with the Artillery School for the use of their athletic grounds every Tuesday and Friday. On the job the recent rains caused the water to rise, and as it was now near the surface, it made the work very dirty. Ties were delivered to the unit the next day and sleepers unloaded from five barges. Six pontoons were assembled and moved from Le Marais to Watten.

Col. Clarke and Major Gibson attended a conference the following day in St. Omer among the Bridge Officers, G.H.Q., French Engineers and Inland Water Transport at which the height for clearance of bridges asked for by the French and the matter of the traffic lines they wished kept open were approved. The party then toured the canal system affected by the road in a launch provided by the I.W.T. As the water level was too high to permit satisfactory work on the Tilques-St. Momelin road on the 8th, arrangements were made to lower the level of water in the Canal. The next day Company Quartermaster Sergeant G. R. Patterson left for England to report to the Royal Air Force, to which he was to be commissioned, and on the next Capt. L. F. Johnston also left for England to train as a pilot with the R.A.F. Facines to reinforce the sides of the formation and also for surface drainage were received. They were placed transversely at intervals of about 25 feet under the ground. On the 13th the planking was started. Although the bridging material had not arrived, the pile driver had been received. A period of dry, hot weather from mid-month now made the conditions of work much more satisfactory, although the calm, moonlight nights gave the enemy ideal opportunities for bombing raids over St. Omer, which received considerable attention. Between 10 p.m. and midnight on the 18th, large numbers of enemy aircraft bombed St. Omer and its environs, hitting a large ammunition dump near Arcques, the blaze illuminating the country for nearly an hour.

Orders the next day called for raising the grade on the Tilques-St. Momelin project to a height of five feet above the level of water in the Canal. The Assistant Director of Light Railways, Second Army, requesting the loan of two survey parties for the location of a proposed light railway from Caestre to the vicinity of Arcques, the matter was referred to Headquarters, Canadian Railway Troops, for approval, and the parties left on the 22nd, under Major Graham. A bomb caused many casualties when enemy aircraft the next day raided St. Omer, caving in the side of No. 10 Canadian Stationary Hospital (Western University), but fortunately none of the patients from the Battalion was injured. Capt. G. B. Little [1] was transferred back to the

On Empire Day, the 23rd, after an inspection of the four companies and the transport after lunch, for it rained in the morning, Gen. Maybury, Director of Roads, took the salute at the march past in column and in close column, with the brass band in attendance. Parchments for decora-unit from the 1st C.R.T., to which he had gone in October, 1916, with more than 300 other ranks. That day planking was completed on half the width of the Tilques-St. Momelin road on the south side, giving a good road in the westerly direction in the event of a withdrawal. Passing sidings had been laid about every 1,000 feet. The bridge party had started driving piles over one large and one smaller bridge, while maintenance continued on the metalled road to Tilques.

---

(1) He was a veteran of the South African War.

tions were presented and the unit marched back to "A" Company Camp through Tilques, led by "D" Company, adjudged the best company on parade. In the evening a concert was given in the Artillery School Cinema, performers being men from the Battalion, the Second Army Artillery School and the two attached labour companies. A film of the trek of the 127th Battalion from Newmarket to Toronto was shown. A programme of sports featured the 24th, but considerable work was done on the projects. The following afternoon, the Battalion team defeated that of the 77th Division, United States Expeditionary Force, in a baseball game by a 7-5 score. Capt. Allan, the Chaplain, left for Etaples the next day on his way to No. 10 Canadian Forestry Company, and was succeeded by Hon. Capt. A. E. Hagar. By that time the unit had nine smaller bridges in course of construction. In the period 27th April to 26th May, the unit located in the Calais area 5.25 miles of standard gauge railway, graded .92 miles, laid .8 miles of steel and ballasted .6 miles. In addition, in the work on roads in the Tilques area, it located 2.75 miles, made .55 miles of location, laid .52 miles of planking and had 12 bridges under construction.

The unit was advised on the 29th that its next task would be the building of a standard gauge railway line from near Watten to Wormhoudt, for which the 55th Chinese Labour Company, the 76th Skilled Chinese Labour Company and the British 38th and 191st Labour Companies would report to the unit on 31st May and 3rd and 4th June. Arrangements would be made to send part of each of the companies of the 2nd C.R.T. to start the work, while the remainder stayed to complete the task of building roads. Accordingly, parties of about a platoon each from "A", "C" and "D" Companies moved on the 31st to the vicinity of the following towns to begin the new projects: "A" Volkerinckhove, "C" Erkelsbrugge and "D" Spreewokt. On Corpus Christi Sunday, 2nd June, the Roman Catholics of the unit, including the recent draft of Russians, attended a church service in Tilques and marched through the town led by the band. In the afternoon in a return game with the American 77th Division baseball team, the unit won again, the 77th band providing music. Orders were received from the Deputy Assistant Director of Roads, VIIth Corps, on the night of 4th June to have ready for traffic the Bois du Ham and Tilques-St.

Momelin roads by the following night, which meant that the planking in one direction must be completed and the bridges decked. To date on the latter road about 4,500 feet of planking had been laid westward from Tilques, but little progress could be made on bridges as the 9-inch by 3-inch decking was still lacking.

Work on the Watten-St. Momelin line was slow that day because of the number of roots encountered and the weight of the material. The French authorities had not yet given sanction to the line running west from the Canal to the Nord Railway line. The next day Capt. J. J. O'Gorman of the Canadian Army Veterinary Corps left the unit to serve as Veterinary Officer of three of the junior battalions of Canadian Railway Troops. The veterinary duties of the 2nd C.R.T. were to be attended to by the Veterinary Officer of the 8th C.R.T. Every effort was made to complete the two plank roads by the evening, the parties starting earlier than usual and working in shifts. The transport section was very busy, as the completion of the work depended on the question of gravel. By 8.15 p.m. the last spike had been driven and the bridges had either been permanently or temporarily decked. At "B" Company's camp the next evening the brass band held a concert, the men of the Company and the 4th Middlesex Labour Company contributing. The talent from the latter company was especially good, as most of them were professional entertainers before the war.

Work on the new Watten-Socx line went fairly well on the 6th, but the lack of data handicapped it. The Engineer Staff furnished the survey parties and several errors appeared, which could have been remedied more quickly if the Battalion's own parties were responsible. The errors were chiefly incorrect marking of grade stakes. As part of the Canadian Railway Troops league schedule, the 8th C.R.T. won a ball game on the Artillery School grounds from the 2nd C.R.T. on Sunday, the 9th, by a score of 22-17. The following day "A" Company moved from Tilques to Spreewokt, leaving a party of 19 under Lieut. Ritchie at a camp near Bridge No. 10 to complete odd jobs on the Tilques road. As the increasing work on the Watten-Socx line required that Battalion Headquarters be closer to it, Major Holdsworth and Capt. Draper, the Quartermaster, searched for a new location, and found Bollezeele, where was situated the unused VIIIth Corps School, the most central place, so an application was made for the use of the buildings, but they were not available.

Col. Clarke and Lieut. Bonn went the next day to look over the Engineer Dump near Strazeele about 500 yards from the front line. The Royal Engineers were forced to evacuate it in recent operations, and before doing so the joints of the rails were blown. Since then efforts had been made to salvage the material, amounting to about 50 miles of steel, 100 switches and quantities of standard gauge and light railway materials. The first method of recovery by a long cable operated by a winch failed, so the Battalion was asked to repair the breaks and bring out the steel by push lorries. For this task, Lieut. Bonn was given charge of 26 other ranks billeted in a farm near Borre. The Chinese Labour Companies did not report for work on the 13th, as it was a national holiday, the Feast of the Dragon. Lieut. Muir was appointed Acting Captain as of 22nd September, 1917. Orders were received on the 14th to widen the tow path of the canal near Tilques, which necessitated a small retaining wall and the removal of the wing kerbs on the road. The 2nd C.R.T. won its second scheduled game in the C.R.T. baseball league against the 10th C.R.T. by a score of 25-1 on the 16th.

By the 20th Battalion Headquarters moved to Bollezeele. Instructions were received to turn over the work on the roads to VIIth Corps. That day Sgts. L. J. Leigh and G. Duckworth and Spr. A. L. Chipman were appointed Temporary Lieutenants. Plans were received the following day for the proposed location of a station yard, supply siding, engineer park and store and ammunition sidings at Zeggers Cappel; supply and ambulance siding at Bollezeele; store and supply sidings, a yard and an engineers stores siding at Lederzeele and a transshipment siding with metre gauge at St. Momelin. The unit was requested the next day to give the Watten end and the St. Momelin transshipping yards the first consideration, as in the event of "certain eventualities" all the stock on the metre gauge railway might need to be evacuated on broad gauge trucks. The 76th

Chinese Labour Company gave a little trouble for a couple of days, as they believed they were overworked. The belief arose because the platoon used one day not proving satisfactory for assisting in laying steel, another was tried the next day. These worked satisfactorily, but conceived the idea that a new platoon was to be provided daily, so they were somewhat rebellious when asked to turn out the following day. Their officers settled the disturbance, however.

In Battalion orders on the 23rd, Temporary Captain (Acting Major) Graham and Acting Capt. Galbraith were promoted Temporary Majors and Temp. Lieuts. Ternan, Muir, Smith and Cameron Temporary Captains. The Acting Director General of Transport, XVth Corps, brought to notice the excellent work of Lieut. Bonn's party and Australian Pioneers in salvaging material from the Strazeele Dump. In one night they salvaged 15 tons of fastenings. On the evening of the 26th, the brass band gave a concert in the Grand Place, Bollezeele. The following day the Russian draft was struck off to four other C.R.T. units. That evening "B" Company's team defeated a baseball team of the Canadian Army Service Corps unit, stationed in the vicinity, and on the afternoon of the 30th the 8th C.R.T. defeated the Battalion team 12-5. In June the unit completed 13.9 miles of standard gauge grade and laid 4.29 miles of steel.

Instructions were received on 2nd July to give priority to the St. Momelin transshipment facilities, to the Zeggers Cappel ammunition and store sidings, to the Zederzeele engineers and store siding and to the St. Momelin supplies siding. In orders that day, Cpl. Hawkins appeared as a Temporary Lieutenant. On the 5th a plan was received of the revised trestle on the Watten chord of the "Y" at the St. Momelin end, consisting of seven bents of nine piles each, accommodating two lines of track. The unit won the next baseball game of the series from the 10th C.R.T. two days later by a 11-0 score, while a few evenings later "B" Company again won from the C.A.S.C. On the St. Momelin end of the work the grading of the yard was continued for 850 feet on the shunting neck and for 300 feet on the track south of the main line. The steel party completed the supply siding, full spiking and plating, and the stem pile driver was enabled to move to the bridge on the Watten leg after replacing two rail lengths and giving the line the necessary lift. The steam driver weighing some 75 tons proved too heavy when it arrived two days previously and went off the track.

A Battalion party of nine signallers began building a telephone line for use in operating the line under construction at the St. Momelin end. A number of non-commissioned officers of the Railway Operating Department arrived from St. Omer to operate the line, and during its construction were to be attached to the unit. Instructions arrived on the 18th to take over the construction of the metre gauge transshipment yard at St. Momelin, and the unit was asked to send a party of 50 other ranks of the 191st Labour Company to the Borre Yard for salvage work, but as that unit was the only white labour attached to the Battalion, and the early completion of the line was required, the order was cancelled for the time being.

Major J. B. Heron was taken on strength on the 20th as supernumerary Major and posted to "B" Company as temporary O.C.; Major Adams reporting to Battalion Headquarters for duty. Plans were received on the 23rd for the water installation in St. Momelin Yard for a 10,000-gallon tank with 2.6 miles of pipe lines to stand-pipes. Water was to be taken from the Canal de L'AA by a Merry-weather pump installed on the canal bank, the Battalion to do all the work. This was turned over to Lieut. Hawkins' party, augmented by pipe fitters from the machine shop. The 8th C.R.T. again defeated the unit the following day in a baseball game. The Engineer Staff Officer notified the Battalion that in the event of necessity it would be responsible for demolishing the bridges on its line. The unit was asked to provide guards the next day for the two metre gauge crossings on the line, and they were provided by the 191st Labour Company. On the ensuing evening the band gave a concert at "A" Company's camp, Loyswick Farm. The monthly survey of work that day showed 12.7 miles of grading, 20 miles of steel laid, 15.5 miles of ballasting and 2.25 miles of grading. From figures then available, the survey party which worked in the Hazebrouck area in June located 23.5 miles.

Unsettled weather with heavy rain at intervals set in for a time, but the work pushed forward. The unit won another baseball game from the 10th C.R.T. by a score of 15-4 on the 28th, when secret instructions arrived for the unit to be responsible for the demolition of certain metre gauge lines in the sector, a task which would extend over about 45 miles of track. Sgt. R. Racine and Cpl. M. Rotelle left on the 29th to go to Canada to serve as instructors for French-Canadian battalions. Major Adams returned from a trip to Sains-en-Amienois where he tried to get news of Sgt. D. R. MacKenzie, wounded at the end of March and of whom nothing had been heard, but without success, although he visited several Casualty Clearing and Dressing Stations. He also placed a cross in the Sains-en-Amienois cemetery over the grave of Lieut. Knox. A General Officer from General Headquarters with the Engineer Staff Officer and Col. Clarke inspected the Watten-Socx line. A party of 16 other ranks boarded medically unfit left that day for the base. Capt. Arthur Bles, Royal Welch Fusiliers, area commandant, Rubrouck, gave a lecture to Headquarters details and "C" and "D" Companies on the subject, "How and why we are winning the war". It was illustrated by maps of the entire front.

On 2nd August a proposed plan of demolition went forward from the 2nd C.R.T. to the Engineer Staff Officer for the metre gauge line from Esquelberg (exclusive) to St. Momelin and for the Bergues-Bollezeele metre gauge line. As many of the culverts noted on the Engineer list were on firm, level ground, and located where in reconstructing the line by a slight diversion requiring little work the obstacle could be avoided, the plan dealt only with structures the demolition of which would retard the enemy advance. Guncotton was asked for only when other explosive could not well be used. The Battalion preferred blastine to ammonal, as it was easier to obtain, familiar to the men, came in convenient cartridges and combined both the lifting and shattering properties of a medium grade dynamite. The unit was not aware whether it was desired to demolish the track itself, but asked for equipment to experiment on salving all rail ahead of the demolition parties. The unit was requested to put in hand the preparation for the demolition of bridges and culverts on these lines and the mining of fills where necessary. Charges might be placed, provided that detonators, primers and fuses were not inserted. Where that was inadvisable, preparation of mine chambers was to be completed and charges stored near the structures, but far enough from the work to safeguard traffic. The 10eme Section Genie Français were for the present responsible for preparation and demolition of track, stations and rolling stock, and also for the actual firing of the structures prepared by the British.

From 1st August, Brig.-Gen. J. W. Stewart, C.M.G., was named to act as Director of Construction, and the Construction Section of the Directorate of Light Railway and the C.A.P.O. were transferred to his control from the 12th. The Battalion tug-of-war championship was won by the Transport section. Four large bombs fell in a field on the Canal de l'AA within 300 yards of the lift bridge, and the enemy showing unusual interest in the operations in the Strazeele Yard, salving was temporarily suspended and the party recalled to "B" Company. To celebrate the fourth anniversary of Britain's entry into the war, the Companies, except "C" and Headquarters, were brought to the Headquarters Camp by train early on the 4th. Capt. Hagar held a church parade, after which the unit paraded through Bollezeele to the transport grounds. After lunch a sports programme was conducted, with guests from the 12th King's Own Yorkshire Light Infantry (Pioneers), who had served with the unit, the 8th and 10th C.R.T., Lt.-Col. Brown and some nursing sisters from the 2nd Canadian Casualty Clearing Station, the Officer Commanding the 3rd Australian C.C.S., Officers from the Engineer Staff, Major Retallack of Headquarters, Canadian Railway Troops, and officers of local units, including attached labour companies. At the tea hour the brass band gave a concert, and at 6.30 p.m. the "Y Emmes" Concert Party another. C.S.M. Price of "C" Company won the medal for highest number of points. Lieut. J. McA. Sharp, wounded near Marcelcave in March, returned and was posted to "D" Company.

A second lecture on the war, this time on the Battle of Verdun, was given on the 8th by Capt. Bles, who took a collection in aid of St. Dunstan's Hospital for the Blind and the French Red Cross. On that day the Canadian Corps in the Amiens sector broke through the enemy positions, pushing forward eight miles. Capt. Bles' final lecture was on the first Battle of Ypres. The 8th C.R.T. baseball team again won by a score of 15-4 against the Battalion team, but the Battalion defeated the football team of the Machine Gun unit. The names of the station group on the Watten-Socx line were changed on the 12th: Zeggers Cappel to Langen, Bollezeele to Smeekaert, Lederzeele to Crome Straat and St. Momelin to La Ferme Bleue. The next day two survey parties were detailed for work under the Assistant Director of Light Railways, one party quartered with the 8th C.R.T. for general land survey on light railways, and the other near Caestre for light railway location. A break caused by a bomb which fell in the night with seven others was repaired on the 22nd. C.S.M. Price and Spr. Walkey won the mile and three miles events in the Railway Operating Department sports on the 25th. The following day the unit started in two trains for Beaucourt in Third Army Area, its strength then being 35 officers, 934 other ranks and 162 horses. The first section (part of Headquarters and "A" and "C" Companies) arrived at Belle Eglise at 9 p.m. and after cutting off the cars of transport continued to Achiet-le Petit, where they remained all night in the train. The transport left early the next morning for Mailly-Maillet, where Battalion Headquarters was to be located. Arriving at Belle Eglise at 3.15 p.m., the second half of the unit left the transport to proceed to Mailly-Maillet and went on to Beausart to march to Battalion Headquarters.

CHAPTER XII

THE ARRAS-ALBERT AREA

With Headquarters and the transport at Mailly-Maillet, "A", "C" and "D" Companies were located in the new area northeast of Miraumont and "B" northeast of St. Pierre Divion, the men chiefly under canvas, although some made use of dugouts and hutting near their camps. The work in hand consisted of the reconstruction of the Arras-Albert standard gauge line from Irles Junction to the southwest to meet the 13th C.R.T., who were working from Albert north, and also the Miraumont-Le Transloy line. Both lines and the bridges had been badly blown. "A", "B", "C" and the 69th Labour Company began clearing the line and the blown bridges on the 28th. Much of the steel was French with rail chairs screwed to the ties, necessitating the use of a special box wrench for removal. A party was put to salvaging a supply of tools. In the preceding month the Battalion had graded on the Watten-Socx line 1.9 miles, repaired a mile of grade, laid 4.25 miles of track, ballasted 12.4 miles and surfaced 15 miles. On the metre gauge line it had graded 4.3 miles, laid 4.3 miles of steel, ballasted 3.5 miles and surfaced 2.2 miles. On the narrow gauge line near Caestre, the special party had located three miles. The next day Major Graham took over the supervision of the bridge construction on the lines. When the technical stores and machine shop arrived the following day at Beausart, as no sidings were available arrangements were made to send the cars to Courcelles crossing.

Instructions arrived to have the Miraumont-Le Transloy line ready to receive a supply train on the early morning of 1st September at La Barque. On the Miraumont-Le Transloy line work was rapid, for few rails had been damaged. The day's work prepared the line for traffic east of the Bapaume road. On the Arras-Albert line some track was prepared except for the bridges, which were unfit for heavy traffic. In the Miraumont yard the spur west of the Cour was repaired to the ramp and the easterly track of the yard repaired and connected with the main line. The Irles "Y" was also cleared and graded for 500 feet. The Miraumont area was heavily shelled during the day by high velocity guns, but there were no casualties, although the new grade at the Irles "Y" was damaged. On the 31st a curious souvenir hunter, tampering with a captured trench mortar, discharged it, the shell bursting against a rail in Miraumont yard, but fortunately no damage was done to anything but the rail itself.

Continuing the repair of the track towards Albert, "C" Company had a particularly difficult task as the rail was of the ball type set in chairs, and as this was the second time it had been hurriedly repaired, it varied in lengths of 32 and 52 feet, which entailed much trolleying back and forth to find unbroken rails to fit. As far as Grandecourt, there were very few evidences of shelling with delayed fuses, the breaks having nearly all been made by the instantaneous type, which, while cutting the rail and destroying the sleeper, did not damage the grade to any extent. While this was probably more by accident than by design, it raised the point that when the British made an advance and shelled a railway to prevent traffic, it would be equally effective to use only instantaneous fuse and so save labour and increase speed in following. When the grade was destroyed it took much time to pump out and fill large craters and almost endless maintenance for months afterwards to keep the line fit for heavy work.

"D" Company continued their work south of the Albert-Bapaume road that day, and at night the first train of ammunition arrived at the La Barque yard, which meant a great saving in long hauls, as that was well up with the guns. "B" Company practically completed grading their section from Grandecourt to Hamel and began laying steel from salvaged rail at points adjacent to places at which they found any quantity of undamaged rails. That section had been heavily shelled by all calibres of guns and it was hard to distinguish any trace of the original line in places. In the course of the next two days, it was expected that the Battalion would link with the 13th C.R.T. at Beaucourt, where a destroyed bridge would prevent either unit from going on until a new one was built.

At noon on 1st September a serious fire was narrowly averted when some canvas in a lorry caught fire and spread to the tarpaulin covering. Quick work by the men nearby pushed other lorries out of reach and tore off the burning canvas, so the loss of the covering and scorching paint was the only result. Roads in the sector were rapidly improving and access could be had to any section by motor transport. The Battalion pushed the completion of the main French Arras-Albert line to meet the 13th C.R.T. and the Miraumont-Le Transloy line rapidly. Both were urgent, but the Le Transloy had priority, as the unit was delivering ammunition right to the battery positions. That line was unique in broad gauge construction, as a 60-pounder battery was located only a few hundred feet from the yard itself. As lines in this sector were not yet handed over to the Railway Operating Department, the Battalion was responsible for operation from Achiet-le Petit exclusive forward and Irles Junction exclusive towards Albert. The Battalion, therefore, made "A" Company responsible for both legs of the "Y" and the main line from Irles Junction to Miraumont, "B" from Grandecourt to the point at which the 13th C.R.T. was met, "C" from Miraumont yard and the main line to Grandecourt and "D" for the Le Transloy line from Miraumont to the end. They were instructed to have pilots accompany trains passing through their sections to warn the guards of any dangerous parts of the line.

Later, the Battalion was instructed to appoint an officer to be responsible for operation of traffic, located at the point at which traffic was taken over from the Railway Operating Department. This officer was to report direct to the Engineer Staff Officer the contents of trains, the time taken over from the R.O.D., time delivered at destination, time emptied and time released by R.O.D. Lieut. H. B. W. Smith was appointed by the unit, so moved to Miraumont to facilitate his handling of trains. In the previous night the enemy resumed shelling the Miraumont area with high velocity guns, doing some damage to "A" and "C" Companies' canvas and hutting from flying splinters. Major Gibson visited the 13th C.R.T. to arrange for their continuing work over the short portion laid by the 2nd C.R.T. and lay a gap for which steel from the Miraumont end could not yet be procured owing to the lack of bridge material. It had been reported that the

13th had timber for the bridge, but Major Gibson found that it and the steel were earmarked for other work and had all been withdrawn from that area.

The 2nd C.R.T. that day received orders to proceed at once with double tracking the Albert-Arras line and to use the undamaged French steel only where it could be brought together and laid in sections of at least a mile in length. Orders also arrived to complete the "Y" at Achiet le Petit. Steel for the Miraumont chord of the Irles "Y" arrived and work began at once, the switch and 1,000 feet of track being laid that day. Teams were employed to haul road metal for the crossing of the road to Achiet le Petit, which then was much used. Maintenance parties were also distributed as usual along the main line putting the track in shape. "B" Company laid steel; completed grading to meet the 13th C.R.T. from Albert, and distributed ties over the line. In the evening the 13th C.R.T. connected their steel with the end of that of the 2nd Battalion. Track on the French main line was repaired and the removal of debris from the Miraumont yard completed. Work began on the 2nd on all the urgent works mentioned, and as "D" Company was operating forward, the tasks were divided among the remaining three. The unit also received another lot of rush works, all of which were required immediately, and with equal priority to the former tasks. These included the La Barque stone spur and a siding and the southernmost of the two dead ends along the Cour at La Barque; a siding at Irles without the 750-foot dead end of the original, and the completion of Miraumont yard and the stone spur at Beaucourt with a siding. Steel laying was completed on the Miraumont chord of the Irles "Y".

Formerly known as "Suicide Corner" and always the subject of intense shell fire, both from British and enemy guns, the Beaucourt Yard, on which the work of clearance continued, was an undesirable mass of twisted steel and splintered wood, churned up and turned over and over until it was almost impossible to clear it. Brig.-Gen. Stewart was a visitor the next day. A misunderstanding had arisen over the section from Beaucourt to Miraumont, as in accordance with instructions to put one track through as soon as possible, the 2nd C.R.T. was to rob the undamaged steel from one side to repair the other. To do that the parties were spread over the whole section repairing what was possible and clearing the debris where it was too badly damaged to make repair possible. In that way a number of detached sections of repaired track occurred with gaps between them. These were regularly reported each afternoon, but when the 13th C.R.T. joined the 2nd C.R.T. section, that unit reported the fact and as they joined on a section of a half-mile, in some way the 2nd C.R.T. reports were apparently not noted, so a wrong impression arose that the line was clear throughout.

The stringers for the six bridges to be built had not yet arrived, but the timber for framing the bents did at noon, so work began at once. Col. Clarke tried to arrange for locomotive power, so far unavailable, as there seemed to be a serious shortage of power in the area and the unit found it almost impossible to handle its traffic in that section, the reason given being shortage of crews. Col. Clarke was told that if he could supply crews, he could have a locomotive at Candas. Although all the experienced men had gone to Audricq, the Battalion made a search among its rank and file for men to tide over the emergency. Col. Clarke also received a new programme of construction made necessary by the change in the tactical situation in front; i.e., the recent British advance. The unit was now to take all men possible from their tasks and concentrate them on the Ligny-Thilloy-Le Transloy line in a great effort to rush steel to Le Transloy yard. Two companies of labour were being moved to a location near Grandecourt. Orders were, therefore, issued to "A" Company to move the next day except for its bridge party, and to "C" to stand by for further instructions. A train crew was sent to Candas to take over a locomotive the following day. Headquarters was also to move forward to a more central point.

Work began that day to clear the grade for the double track from Irles Junction southward. A rough reconnaissance of the new line on the 4th revealed much heavier work than expected. Four heavy cuts and three heavy fills had only been scratched before the enemy occupation and nothing more had been done on them since. A forward camp site for headquarters was located, and an advance party was sent with the Sanitary Section to prepare it and to bury the dead remaining in the vicinity since its capture a few days previously. Orders came to build a spur for a Casualty Clearing Station at Beaulencourt for transshipment to lorries and to push the double track from Irles Junction to Miraumont. All this made such a large amount of priority work on hand that it would be difficult to carry it through with success, with the lack of labour promised but not yet arrived. A party of 105 other ranks of "A" Company under Lieut. MacDonald went to Ligny-Thilloy to begin grading the line to Le Transloy, half a mile being completed. A frog and guard rails were salvaged and laid and switch rails from Miraumont were to be placed on arrival the next day. A bridge party of eight with Sgt. Calder remained at the old camp at Miraumont to complete the bridges, and the remainder of the company moved to a new camp at Goudecourt. Work also began on the Irles siding, urgently needed before moving forward. Grading there was not heavy, but several craters, one very large, took nearly all the work that day.

Battalion Headquarters moved early the following day from Mailly Maillet to its new location near Ligny-Thilloy. The 13th and 138th Labour Companies reported in the evening minus tools, which were secured during the night by lorry. Orders were received that the Casualty Clearing Station spur was only to be built when it would not interfere with other urgent work. Every available man of "A" Company was placed on grading and laying the switch at the junction of the Le Transloy line. All teams on the company strength were used on ploughing scraper work on two large fills on which a great deal of work was required, as the ground was torn with shell holes and baked so hard little progress could be made until the surface was removed. Grading in the heavy cuts and fills west of Le Transloy went slowly through the undulating country because of the great number of shell holes almost lip to lip, making it difficult to move much yardage until the borrow was opened, when it became possible to employ more teams. The unit requested an additional 25 teams for a week.

Steel laying on the Le Transloy line by "A" Company's parties began on the 6th. Because of recent regulations requiring the immediate relinquishment of rail carrying cars, all steel had to be unloaded at the junction and reloaded on track lorries to be hauled to the end of steel. Word arrived the next day that the Railway Operating Department was taking over operation of the line as far as Miraumont yard, inclusive. The remaining area under operation by the unit now included Miraumont exclusive to Beaucourt, and Beaulencourt exclusive to Beaulencourt and towards Le Transloy. With his operating staff, Lieut. Smith moved forward to Miraumont Junction. Instructions were received to proceed to place the double track bridges on the line from Miraumont to Beaucourt. The order for the material was already in, and in fact at the bridge at the south end of Miraumont yard, where the line crossed a road the bent placed for the single line was doubled, only requiring the stringers to complete it as a double track bridge. Poor progress was made that day in steel laying, as an empty supply train could not be pulled out for lack of power and was set on the Le Transloy line, cutting "A" Company off from its steel supply. All the Company had as a result was a few undamaged salvaged rails.

On the following afternoon 23 other ranks and 41 mules arrived from the 4th C.R.T. in response to the Battalion's request for more transport to complete its earth work before the steel came. The latter was now arriving without fittings. Reconnaissance of the forward lines was completed that night as far as the Sorel road crossing near Hendecourt. The single track line from Albert to Arras was completed and opened for traffic where the gaps over the bridges were laid that day. The stone spur and siding at Beaucourt was also completed. Rain fell intermittently for three days, and while the steel parties carried on, it hampered their work and increased the danger of derailment, while the earth work became heavy and the footing was poor. After two hours' work on the 12th the teams had to be recalled.

Orders not to expend labour in trimming and surfacing the French main Albert-Arras line other than what was necessary to put it into good running condition were received the next day, as the French were following behind the 2nd C.R.T. building permanent bridges and laying their own steel. Instructions also arrived verbally to locate a stone spur near Battalion Headquarters camp to be used temporarily for stabling the Army Commander's train. Several Staff Officers visiting the location party approved of it, as it ran through a lane in a grove of trees serving to hide the train effectually. Numerous warnings as to the action of enemy mines and explosives were received the following day. One about Perdite cited an instance in which after it was removed from danger and placed in a field, it exploded either from delayed action or from spontaneous combustion. All this information was passed to the men on the line, who were continually finding and removing unexploded mines. The double track on the Albert-Arras line was completed and opened to traffic that day. As material was not as long in coming, the second line was repaired much more quickly than the first. The earth work on Le Transloy line was also completed, the teams working 12 hours. As the cuts were so narrow as to be only sufficient to permit the passing of a train, the unit began widening them where steel was not up by using 60-centimetre tip trucks, and when the trucks passed this point by the use of a "mud train" and locomotive, widening the fills with the spoil.

A census of all rolling stock on the unit lines taken on the 15th by R. S. M. Jowett was hampered by the congestion of traffic in Achiet le Grand Yard and the consequent diversion of incoming trains to Miraumont, with the result that it also became congested and affected the whole system as well, so empty trains could not be cleared. At 10 a.m. the unit had more than 490 cars on the line, entailing heavy work to check, every available siding being blocked. Two days later the unit was advised that it was being supplied with five locomotives with double crews stabled with the Battalion continuously and not for the day only as with the two already in use, for the purpose of speeding the removal of ballast from the pit at Miraumont.

Instructions now called for the unit to continue track laying until it linked with the 12th C.R.T., which was laying steel westward from Etricourt. The 2nd C.R.T. was also to rebuild the yard at Le Transloy and repair the spurs running to the southeast. At Rocquigny the tracks to be installed were the main line, the first loop north of it and the spur along the west side of the Rocquigny-Mesnil road. The 12th

C.R.T. was to rebuild the Etricourt Yard and the loop at Mesnil was to be installed by whichever working party reached it first. It was essential that the track be ballasted and in good condition to Le Transloy on the night of the 19th. The Engineer Staff was notified that the 148th Labour Company at Grandecourt, the 69th and Butte de Warlencourt and the 65th near Le Transloy could be called on in an emergency for work other than that of the 2nd C.R.T. By bright moonlight, the unit ran ballast that night until 11 p.m., when the supply at Miraumont was exhausted, in the period between trains the men being employed in shovelling the ballast into the truck ready for the ballast parties to begin lifting and packing in the morning, by which means 2,100 feet was filled. Steel laying on the stone spur at Ligny Thilloy was completed at 3 p.m. ready for the Army Commander's train.

This train arrived that night and was placed in position at 4.30 a.m. under the supervision of Major Gibson. As the cars were rigidly coupled and some rolled on three sets of bogies, it was very difficult to move them over the new track without derailment. A memorandum from the Officer Commanding the 69th Labour Company on the 18th advised the Battalion that he had had an urgent detail from the Labour Commandant, Vth Corps, to send 75 other ranks to Bapaume that day, which not only prevented the unit from carrying out its programme of running ballast that night, but was an injustice to the men who had worked all the previous night. Orders arrived for the unit to move to Roisel for work in that area by way of Chemin Verte and Chaulnes. In the Miraumont yard both approaches to the tank ramp were completed and in the Beaulencourt Casualty Clearing Station spur the first lift with mine earth was 60 per cent completed. On the Le Transloy line with 225 cars of ballast that work was pushed forward, and on the Arras-Albert line more surfacing of the double track line was done.

By 10 a.m. the next morning, the Battalion was packed, leaving small parties behind at the various company camps to continue work with the labour until the 13th C.R.T. took over the lines. At 1 p.m. the mechanical transport carrying Headquarters stores moved off by road under Lieut. Thomas and the horse transport under Lieut. MacDonald assembled at Le Transloy, moving off by road. At 10.30 p.m. the locomotives arrived to take the first train under Major Craig and soon moved. The rear party of 24 of "B" Company with 295 of the 148th Labour Company continued the maintenance in the Miraumont yard and surfaced the double track, while "A" Company's rear party and attached labour continued ballasting on the Miraumont-Le Transloy line, and "D" Company's detachment of 40 and attached labour worked at the Rocquigny Yard, completing the through siding, the switch track and the spur on the north side of the main line, and also connected the latter to meet the 12th C.R.T. at the road crossing at the east end of the yard.

CHAPTER XIII

THE ROISEL-ST. QUENTIN LINE

Battalion Headquarters was located in a former British camp at Montigny Farm, an officer from each company accompanying the advance party to select sites for camps close to the work, which was the reconstruction of the Roisel-St. Quentin line. The mechanical transport arrived at 9 p.m., the horse transport at 4 a.m. on the 20th and the first train with "C" and "D" Companies and the technical stores reached Roisel four hours later. "C" Company was located near Roisel and "D" near Vendelles. As all the unit's positions were in the area containing the heavy artillery, dugouts and iron shelters were used as far as possible, but the technical stores remained at Roisel until a siding was available on the line. The work of construction of the Roisel-St. Quentin line to follow possible advances towards the latter town would be hard. The Germans had built the line from Roisel to Montigny Farm only and from Montigny to Vermand it was in the same condition as in September, 1917. Charges had been placed against most of the joints, but many had not exploded. From Montigny to Vermand there were neither rails nor sleepers, while the formation, which had been used as a pathway or road, was in the same condition as a year previously. Four arches or bridges had all been demolished.

The work of the unit also included the reconstruction of the southwest leg of the "Y" at Roisel to accommodate a 14-inch railway gun, which necessitated closer spacing of the ties and more ballasting. The next day "C" and "D" Companies began work on the line. On the eastern leg of the Roisel "Y" 1,600 feet of the old steel was removed and 700 feet of new relaid. On the west leg the steel was complete, the only work required being the clearance of debris from the line preparatory to ballasting. The switch at the junction of the two legs was installed and on the main St. Quentin line all debris was removed as far south as the entrance to Montigny Yard. An officer of the Royal Engineers arrived with a special machine for unscrewing coach screws from the plates. "D" Company's parties laid 1,200 feet of track preparatory to clearing a cut. The train with Headquarters and "A" and "B" Companies reached Roisel at 10 p.m., the men remaining in it overnight because of the late hour, and marched to their new camps the following morning, "A" near Headquarters at Montigny Farm and "B" near the Sugar Refinery. An Engineering Battalion of the 30th American Division and half the 168th Labour Company reported for duty that day.

Brig.-Gen. Stewart with Col. MacDonell of his staff visiting the unit on the 23rd asked for the building of a mile of steel a day on the Roisel-St. Quentin line. With the 168th Labour Company, "C" Company's parties continued removing the old steel for 6,000 feet southeast to the beginning of the Montigny Yard and also 400 feet in the yard itself, the work being much simplified by the new screw-drawing machine. A total of 700 feet of new steel was laid and on the west arm of the "Y" at Roisel surplus ballast was removed. The first steel and ballast train reached Roisel at 4 p.m. "A" Company's parties were engaged in Montigny Yard preparing the grade for the main line. Capt. Ternan and Lieut. MacDonald took out "A" Company's bridge parties to begin building two timber bridges. "B" Company's parties removed 400 feet of light railway in the yard of Montigny Farm and continued clearing the right of way for 1,700 feet southeast. Scraper teams were used to fill in a mine crater just east of the point at which the clearing stopped. A culvert was to be installed in this crater. "D" Company's parties continued on the line between Vendelles and Vermand, completing a temporary trestle and excavations for abutments for bents for a bridge, and filling craters with scrapers and mule teams.

Early the following morning enemy aircraft bombed the neighbourhood of the Company Camps, but no damage was done, although several bombs fell unpleasantly close to the technical stores in Roisel yard. Enemy shell fire destroyed a road crossing in the early morning, however. The Engineer Battalion of the 30th American Division started work that morning, but unfortunately was recalled after working only three-quarters of an hour, but in that time they did as much work as the Battalion usually expected from Pioneers or

Labour in six times that period. "C" Company and attached labour laid 2,500 feet of steel. It had been hoped to lay a mile of steel, but the expected locomotive failed to arrive, so the steel had to be hauled by push lorries. The removal of old steel was continued and ballasting began on the southwest leg of the Roisel "Y", 800 feet being lifted. Owing to the considerable amount of ballast required for the spur, the ballast on the ground and the 19 cars received that day were insufficient to complete the work.

A party of about 100 of "A" Company was employed in Montigny yard clearing the grade for the main line and grading on the last track of the yard. The old German steel was entirely cleared from two of the tracks. The remainder of the company worked on the preparation for the foundations of two of the bridges. On "B" Company's section of the line south of Montigny, the track was cleared and the grade prepared for 1,400 feet easterly. Five mule teams with scrapers completed filling the crater mentioned previously. While helping clear the grade, Sgt. Tack of "B" Company was injured by the explosion of a bomb lying unnoticed among the rubbish. "D" Company was also employed in filling craters. The Company's camp was subjected to shell fire intended for the nearby batteries, but no harm was done. Early on the 25th bombing from enemy aircraft was heavy near Battalion Headquarters, one bomb dropping in "C" Company's camp but doing no damage beyond destroying several articles of clothing, as the tents were protected for a height of about two feet by sand bags. Later in the day the neighbourhood of Montigny Yard was periodically shelled, but the only casualty was Spr. W. V. Conning of "B" Company, slightly injured by a splinter.

Continuing to lay steel and ballast, "C" Company and the 168th Labour Company had to manhandle or draw the steel by mules as the locomotive failed to report. A total of 4,000 feet was laid to the southeast and 200 feet from the Roisel end of the east leg of the "Y" to the switch crossover. As no ballast arrived, the party was employed in packing and shouldering the southwest leg of the "Y". A small party of "A" Company continued clearing the main line grade in Montigny Yard and in grading track there. Part of the company at Vermand, increased to 92 other ranks, carried on the work on the bridge abutments, the timber for which had just arrived at Roisel. In "B" Company's sector, ballast was cleared from the yard and the mine crater filled, and the dirt and dugouts were cleared from the cuts and the road crossing cleared at the east end of Montigny Yard. "D" Company continued filling three craters, using tip cars of the light railway. Bombing in the early hours of the following morning and shelling during the day continued near Montigny Farm and near "D" Company's camp, that company being forced to leave camp again and move into the railway cutting.

Advice was received that four labour companies totalling about 1,150 would report to the Battalion shortly. Steel laying was made easier that day by the help of a light railway locomotive and six flat cars and the long expected standard gauge locomotive. The remainder of "A" Company moved from Montigny to a new location in dugouts, since a canvas camp would have been impossible, as it would have been under direct observation. At Miraumont, Capt. Ternan salvaged about 200 pounds of German explosives with fuses and detonators to use in clearing away part of the bridge abutments at Vermand, the brick and stone being too hard for ordinary picks and cold sets. The foundation of that bridge was completed and now awaited the timber sections. That day 3,500 feet of steel was laid. It was reported that in the previous month 3.1 miles of line had been located, 7.05 miles graded, 12.3 miles of grade repaired, 30.3 miles of track laid and 8.4 miles ballasted.

A special party was detailed by "C" Company the next day to stay near the gun spur, which was the southwest leg of the Roisel "Y", to make repairs to the track as the occasion arose, while the 14-inch gun placed there that day was in operation. The labour units promised began arriving, the 12th Labour Company allotted to "A" Company, the 114th to "B", the 14th to "C" and the 6th Middlesex (Alien) was yet to come. In the Montigny Yard 2,400 feet was laid on No. 2 siding and a switch and siding 750 feet long laid for the technical stores cars, while the grading of No. 1 track continued. Clearing the grade and widening cuts was carried on over the line at various points and sleepers were distributed ahead of the work, while "B" Company laid 1,500 feet of steel. The excavation for the overhead bridge on "D" Company's section was 75 per cent complete. "C" Company graded 500 feet of No. 1 Spur in Montigny Yard on the 28th, laid 1,000 feet of steel, distributed a mile of sleepers and installed a switch on No. 3 siding. The Company's detachments also carried on maintenance on the Roisel gun spur. "B" Company continued clearing the grade of ballast and rubbish, laying 2,300 feet of steel to the southeast, and distributed sleepers hauled by mule teams. The three large craters on "D" Company's section were nearly filled and the excavation for the bents of the bridge was 90 per cent complete. Their parties cleared 2,600 feet of old ballast from the grade. That morning the bridge timbers arrived at Montigny and transshipment to the site of the work near Vermand was started. Because of a difference in sizes from that expected, careful calculation would be necessary.

At 5.30 a.m. on the 29th a heavy British barrage north of St. Quentin announced another offensive. In Battalion Orders that day a letter was quoted conveying the thanks of the Director of Construction for the manner in which broad gauge construction was carried out in the Third and Fourth Army areas in the recent advances, and for the "unparalleled progress made". Over "C" Company's section ballasting was done for 10,200 feet, that amount being possible because of the good condition of the existing road bed. In Montigny Yard 300 feet of grading was done on the track, two large dugouts being removed and two smaller ones shifted, while the steel at the north end of No. 1 track was converted to the spur. "B" Company's parties cleared the ballast from the line and earth from the cut to permit laying steel through it; distributed ties to the southeast, and laid 2,400 feet of steel in that direction. The 114th Labour Company began working with "B". In "D" Company's section one large crater was filled and another almost completed, as were also the excavations for the bridge, with the help of the 14th Labour Company. The movement of bridge timbers by waggons from Montigny was finished, and "A" Company's bridge was already 25 per cent complete. The crater at Vermand Station was 60 per cent completed and about 2,000 feet of ballast was removed along that section. Shelling began again near the grade opposite Vermand at 10.30 a.m. The 6th Middlesex (Alien) Labour Company arrived the following day and was detailed to "C" Company's advance detachment, which moved ahead of "A" Company's section at Vermand, as their work would shortly be in advance.

On 1st October the personnel of the Battalion learned that Bulgaria had accepted the peace terms. At midnight on the 31st/1st, the new 24-hour system became effective, doing away with the previous designations "a.m." and "p.m." By this date, the end of steel on the Roisel St. Quentin line was half-way between Vendelles and Vermand. One bridge was complete, the work of filling the craters was well advanced and the passing siding at Montigny Farm was finished and connected with the main line. "A" Company was then at Vermand, "B" near Montigny Farm, "D" at Vendelles and "C" moved that day from near Roisel to the vicinity of Marteville. The next day an experiment in moving steel forward by lorries and pontoon tractors was made by Gen. Holman, "Q", Fourth Army. It was desired to move steel for Savy Yard before the construction of the main line and build the yard by the time the line was connected. Motor lorries were used for hauling two pontoon waggons on which six rails were loaded, but it was found that the tractors could not stand the rough roads and the weight of steel. During the day about 17 trips were made. Steel laying on the main line continued, 4,700 feet being laid to a point just south of Bihecourt Station. In Montigny Yard 75 feet was added to the supply siding. In the evening Majors Holdsworth and Graham went to St. Quentin to see the canal bridge, which had a span of 80 feet and was blown and rebuilt by the Germans. In the recent operations they dropped the iron beams, which hung on the abutments with the ends lying in the canal. The centre bents were 22 feet from the south abutment and were 14 feet apart. That day "D" Company moved to Holnan Wood.

A total of 5,200 feet of steel to a point near Vermand Station was laid the following day, while a bridge was completed and at Montigny Yard a party repaired the ramp and filled craters ahead of steel. Work on the long cuttings through Holnan Forest progressed slowly. Destroyed in the withdrawal of the enemy in 1917 and not repaired during the French or the British occupation, it was used as a dugout area by the latter. From the Forest forward a heavy gradient to the Canal was under direct fire from the enemy lines, so the work had to be done quietly with small parties. The weather on the 4th although cloudy and damp gave cover from enemy observation. The bridge party of "B" Company under Lieut. MacPherson started to rebuild the bridge over the Canal at St. Quentin spanning the canal and the Somme River, which ran side by side and were only separated by a flume. Originally a truss, the bridge was destroyed and rebuilt by the Germans using six 24-foot "I" beams for the south span, supported by a timber tower founded on the flume. When he retreated, the enemy mined the tower, dropping the end of the "I" beams into the river, but otherwise no damage was done to them. He also had begun preparations for demolition in each abutment, but these were removed and no damage resulted. The Battalion's method of repairing the structure was to erect a new tower on the flume and raise the "I" beams into position again. Enemy observation, however, was good at this point. Plans for the reconstruction of the ambulance spur at Bihecourt were sent to "A" Company that day, and on the next the latter started grading for it, completing 35 per cent of the grade. At Montigny "B" Company's parties completed four sidings and the ramp, while on the main line steel was pushed farther forward and in the yard at Vermand 900 feet was laid.

Two companies working on steel laying in 6-hour shifts on the 6th pushed the end of steel to a point near Attilly, while "A" Company and the 12th Labour Company worked on the ambulance spur, Bihecourt, and graded the main line, and other parties were employed in filling craters and clearing cuts. Through Holnan Forest the spoil was so deep that as a preliminary only a narrow cutting could be put through it, leaving the work of widening to later parties with mud trains. The soil was a peculiar mixture of sand and clay, and after the rains began to slide in at points, making it necessary to patrol the section continually. The bridge party at St. Quentin was dismantling the canal bridge as far as the fallen bents were concerned. That evening a non-commissioned officer of "B" Company was shot through the knee by an unknown French soldier from a nearby

French camp who entered the corporal's dugout and tried to sell a German revolver, which was accidentally fired. The French soldier then disappeared without trace. "B" Company moved that day to an old quarry near Francilly-Selency. Dull weather helped the work the next day, as clear days gave the enemy observation both on the St. Quentin bridge and on the line east of Holnan. At Montigny Farm all steel required to date was laid and the ambulance siding at Bihecourt was ready for traffic that night, although lacking in ballast. In the Vermand Yard No. 1 track was laid ready for use as well as the passing loop.

Steel laying the following day reached the cut through Savy Wood, but there the shortage of labour made itself felt, and the cut could not be cleared of spoil and broken rail fast enough to keep the track layers going constantly. At 4.30 a.m. that morning the Third British Army attacked, accompanied by a demonstration by artillery on the Canadian Corps front, in the operations preceding the capture of Cambrai. This spoiled the enemy's observation on both the track and the bridge at St. Quentin, so work on the latter started actively without the usual interruptions. At Bihecourt the ambulance siding was completed and 900 feet of steel laid on the main line, and between Roisel and Vermand ballasting was finished and near Savy the cut was prepared for steel. The previous night enemy bombers were active, dropping bombs near "A", "B" and "D" Companies, but doing little damage. On the 9th tracklaying was again impeded by the failure of the labour to clear the line of damaged rails, but steel was laid to the junction of the single track line from Ham to Savy Wood. The general location for the Fourth Army Commandant's train was decided on and work started at once, as it was required for the 12th. The first ambulance passed over the Bihecourt spur in the morning, Col. Clarke himself superintending it. Brig.-Gen. Stewart, Col. MacDonell and Lieut.-Col. Anderson, Engineer Staff Officer, Fourth Army, were visitors, the latter making a tour of St. Quentin yard with Major Gibson and Capt. Ternan to decide what lines would be used as a railhead. He then left to confer with Commandant Tesseraud of the French Engineers.

Beyond a few shell and bomb holes, St. Quentin Yard was still intact. The enemy evidently intended salvaging the steel, but was interrupted before he could blow the joints. He seemed to have felt secure in proprietorship, as he erected a glaring signboard on the station: "German Military Railway." At Holnan-Savy siding 1,500 feet of steel was opened for traffic and the passing siding at Bihecourt also completed for operations. In the Savy-Ost Yard (formerly German) a big crater was filled ready to take one track. In the evening a telephone message relayed a General Headquarters priority wire to place St. Quentin Yard in condition for four trains daily from and including 14th October, so all work in Bihecourt Yard was called off for the time being. Two platoons of "A" Company moved the following day to the brick yard near St. Quentin, and the remaining two continued the work of lifting in Bihecourt Yard, as well as offloading and shipping forward by lorries the timber required for the St. Quentin bridge. In the Holnan-Savy yard 3,000 feet of steel was laid and in the Savy-Ost yard the crater was filled to accommodate four tracks. Word arrived that evening that the unit was to work with the French on reconstruction from the St. Quentin Yard forward. The remainder of "A" Company moved to the brick yards the next day, leaving only a small rear party of about 20 to maintain the line near Vermand.

The French linked with the St. Quentin Yard at 1700 hours on the 12th, their first locomotive rolling into the town blowing its whistle for several minutes. The 2nd C.R.T. followed closely and at 1730 "B" Company linked with "A" Company's section, completing steel between Roisel and Rocourt Yard, only the St. Quentin Canal lying between the Battalion and the St. Quentin Yard. The bents of the bridge were up and the hoisting of the "I" beams could be started the next morning. The Railway Operating Department was providing a steam crane for the purpose. The spur for the Army Commandant's train was all but complete. At 2 a.m. the next morning the unit was informed that a rear end collision had occurred on the line between Roisel and Montigny just outside the latter station. An ambulance train was closely followed by a troop train with engine front and rear, the former either going very slowly or stopped, and as the night was dark and it was claimed no rear light was lit, the troop train ran into it. The rear engine of the latter not hearing any signal to stop, kept on moving, so several cars of that train were telescoped, causing the deaths of 13 and injury to about 30. As this part of the line was under the Railway Operating Department, it took the investigation in hand. The 2nd C.R.T. maintenance parties set to at once to extricate the injured and clear the line, which was done by early daylight in a drizzle of rain.

Little work was required in repairing tracks in St. Quentin Yards west of the bridge as little steel had been damaged. That night the unit was instructed to meet the French at 0700 hours the next day and begin work on the line from St. Quentin to Bohain, one party at the St. Quentin end and the other in Essigny Yard. The British desired a railhead at Busigny and as that was in the French area they asked for help in building it. In addition, the Battalion was allotted a bridge over the Fonsomme-Fontaine-Uterts road. From the east end of the French yard at St. Quentin to the beginning of Essigny Station, no demolitions of track had been carried out, all breaks having been caused by shell fire. All turnouts and some rails in Essigny had been demolished. The overhead Decauville crossing, a brick arch, had been demolished, leaving a barrier of brickwork about six feet high and 14 feet wide. The overhead bridge on the road from St. Quentin to Homblières had a brick abutment completely destroyed, dropping the roadway across both tracks; while the overhead bridge on the St. Quentin-Fontaine-Notre Dame road was in similar condition. The underbridge on the Omissy-Morcourt road with trough girders in brick abutments had one of the latter damaged on the corner by a shell, making it necessary either to cut down the brickwork and rebuild it with timber or to support the girder with a trestle of two posts or more.

The entire Bohain Station had been systematically demolished and also the track for a distance south. In the station there were no large craters, but several mines appeared to have been prepared at the road crossings, but had not exploded. With few exceptions, the rails had been blown at the joints and all points and crossings demolished, while the building had also been deliberately wrecked, including the water tower tanks and the fittings. The enemy had made various alterations in the station, which with part of the line was only captured on the 10th, but it was evident that the railway had been destroyed for several weeks. A metre gauge over one bridge had been totally wrecked, the steelwork lying across the line and about 300 cubic feet of debris requiring removal. Likewise a road bridge was entirely destroyed, requiring much clearing before it would be possible to rebuild it to get the road down to its proper level. A large transshipment station had been built about 800 yards west of Bohain Station.

A Maintenance Company under Major Graham was organized in the Battalion on the 14th, consisting of approximately one officer and 15 other ranks from each company, to take over completion of lines and their maintenance, enabling the companies on construction to move forward and keep up with the advances of the Army. In Bihecourt Yard 1,500 feet of steel was laid on the stone siding and in Savy Ost Yard 700 feet of siding laid. Rocourt Yard was cleared of damaged steel and the erection of St. Quentin bridge was 90 per cent completed. Half of "C" Company moved to Essigny. The next day saw the finishing of the St. Quentin bridge, a difficult task. The girders were 56 feet long and weighed some five tons each. It was originally planned to pull them up with a winch and gin poles, but the lower ends were so firmly embedded in brick debris that instead a 35-ton wrecking crane was used. When the latter arrived the boom was too short, as was that of the 15-ton machine which was sent later, so the only use which could be made of them was to pull the girders out of their bed and hold them while the winch elevated them into place, a slow process requiring about an hour of hard winding. When the long girders were in position, it was simple to place the short ones, as the crane was able to seize them at the point of balance and swing them directly into place. "A" Company began work on one of the destroyed bridges with timber brought to Rocourt Yard by train and thence by lorries. With the completion of the St. Quentin bridge, steel was connected with the St. Quentin Yards by 1600 hours and the Yards opened for traffic. On the line northeast towards Le Cateau, one section was completed except for three bridge spans to be removed by crane. In Bihecourt Yard the passing loop was opened for traffic, as was also an 1,800-foot siding at Savy.

CHAPTER XIV

ST. QUENTIN-BOHAIN

Obstructions on the line to Bohain were removed by the 35-ton crane used on the St. Quentin bridge on 15th October. At points near the village of Rouvroy two bridges of reinforced concrete had been blown by the enemy, who mined the brick abutments, causing the floors to fall to the track below intact. To break them would take time and labour, so the crane was brought and easily cleared them. On the line in front of St. Quentin clearing was done to the north of Morcourt Yard, while in the Savy Ost Yard a siding 2,300 feet long was opened for traffic. At Rocourt a spur of 1,300 feet north of the main line was made ready for traffic and two sidings were cleared, and at Essigny on No. 3 track of the yard 2,085 feet of steel was completed and 5,300 feet on No. 4 track. "C" Company's parties removed defective steel there, but little work was necessary as little damage was done. "D" Company's survey party began retracing the line from Roisel to Holnan. The following day on the St. Quentin-Busigny line steel was opened to a point between Remaucourt and Essigny le Petit, as well as on various sidings on the main line. At Rocourt Yards three sidings west from St. Quentin bridge were repaired and at Essigny Yard the old destroyed track was dismantled. "D" Company's parties began ballasting the stone siding at Bihecourt. A board of enquiry consisting of Major Graham and Lieuts. Thomas and Davis was convened to investigate a collision between the "D" Company mud train and a light engine at Vermand two nights previously. Capt. W. A. Chadwick, Canadian Army Pay Corps, arrived to replace Capt. Marshall, who left for England.

Steel was opened through to a point just northeast of Essigny le Petit on the St. Quentin-Bohain line the next day. In Rocourt Yard 200 feet of steel was laid in sidings, and at Bihecourt the stone spur was completely ballasted. At Essigny, 1,800 feet of the old steel was taken from No. 1 track, and switches already prepared were ballasted. That night the Engineer Staff Officer, Fourth Army, wired for either Col. Clarke or Major Gibson to meet him at 1030 hours on the 18th at Essigny Station to interview Commandant Tesseraud of the French Army Engineers, because of the French belief that one of the Battalion's bridges would delay their track laying. At the conference the French party accepted an invitation to visit the bridge and judge for themselves. On arrival they found the last sleepers being laid on the deck all ready for the steel, which was still kilometres away, so expressed themselves satisfied and were surprised to find the second bridge for the double track in an advanced stage of construction. Up to dark the previous night, the French had not yet reached the structure, so the diarist comments: "Considerable annoyance is felt that so much unnecessary trouble has been caused by inexperienced men passing judgment on the progress."

An outcome of the conference was that the 2nd C.R.T. was allotted two other sections of the work; from Bohain exclusive of the yard to Busigny exclusive from the yard, and from Busigny exclusive of the yard to Honnechy including the yard, with instructions to work towards Cambrai from the junction at Busigny to meet the 4th C.R.T. coming from that place. It appeared that the French did not wish the Canadians to do any work in either Bohain or Busigny yards, as they preferred to repair their signal system when repairing the yard. A reconnaissance of the section from Busigny to Honnechy was then made, but it revealed little to be done, since although the line had been prepared for demolition, it had never been carried out. In Rocourt Yard 1,700 feet of steel was laid ready for traffic on the passing loop, while "B" Company completed a tank for supplying locomotives water at St. Quentin.

Half of "A" Company was moved by lorry to a new camp under canvas near Busigny on the 20th. In the Bohain Yard broken rails were replaced and damaged steel was removed. Working south from Busigny towards Bohain, "D" Company had a formidable task, as about 80 per cent of the track had been destroyed and three large and a number of small craters had to be filled. Working in Bohain Yard the preceding week, a company of the Royal Engineers sawed the ends off 4,000 feet of damaged track and relaid it, but only bored one hole in each end, so if it were to be used, a great deal of drilling was required. If other steel could be obtained, it was decided not to use it, as the varying lengths made it unsuitable for a yard in an area subject to bombing, for the action of concussion near a rail tended to render it liable to breaking under traffic owing to crystallization. Rain for two days caused some trouble in the cuts along the Roisel-St. Quentin line, so extra labour was asked for to put it in condition to carry a 14-inch American gun shortly expected. In Essigny Yard "C" Company was greatly hampered by the French, "who change their minds on matters of procedure with great rapidity," a condition especially marked with switches.

The work on the St. Quentin-Busigny line was taken over by the 2nd C.R.T. from the 263rd Company, Royal Engineers, the following day with the labour of that company, including the 83rd and 90th Labour Companies and the 78th Burmese Labour Company. The work of clearing and repairing the Le Cateau line was pushed forward towards Honnechy. Work was done also on the road bridge with the overhead brick arch completely dropped over the line, and in Essigny Yard with the French 3,600 feet of steel was laid on two tracks. At 1630 hours one of the 76 Skilled Chinese Labour Company without apparent provocation struck one of the Company's officers on the head with a pick. The Chinese disappeared and the officer was removed to a nearby Casualty Clearing Station with a fractured skull. That day "D" Company moved from Savy to Bohain. Debris clearing on the Le Cateau and Cambrai line continued the next day, the line being little damaged. In Bohain Yard 900 yards of broken steel was removed, and the debris of the overhead bridge taken from the line. To be nearer the work at Fresnoy le Grand, a platoon of "D" Company with labour moved there that day. "A" and "C" Companies found a ten-acre field of cabbage near Busigny, as if in return for the garden the unit "presented to the enemy" at Cugny the previous March.

Col. Clarke and Major Gibson went to Le Cateau on the 23rd to view the destroyed viaduct, a structure some 800 feet long and 70 high, and totally destroyed except for two piers. The unit planned to send a party to make a location to avoid it by using an old enemy metre gauge line climbing from the valley of the Essart into Le Cateau. That was the only alternative, as the country to the south towards St. Souplet was too broken. On the Busigny-Le Cateau line, repairs were made to Honnechy Yard, in which a party was engaged removing an enemy ammunition train destroyed by shell fire. From Busigny to Bohain steel laying continued, the east track being stripped to repair the other track. Filling craters also continued, slip scrapers being used. Of the ten craters along this section of track, 60 per cent were ready for single track that night. In Bohain Yard parties began removing the debris of the fallen bridge, and a 60-centimetre track was repaired for filling craters. At Fresnoy le Grand the 90th Labour Company was employed in dismantling damaged steel. Steel was laid the following day on the Bohain-Busigny line and on the main road west of the latter. In Honnechy Yard clearing was completed and four tracks were made ready for traffic. Switches were repaired and the track built by the enemy removed for rebuilding the other damaged lines. In Fresnoy le Grand two tracks were opened for traffic and ballasting and lining were done. The remainder of "C" Company moved from Essigny to Fresnoy le Grand.

While looking through Le Cateau Yard Capt. Ternan discovered a German standard gauge inspection car with a Mercedes engine of about 30 horse power practically undamaged, so arrangements were made to use it. That evening the well-known Canadian poet, Robert W. Service, was a visitor. The next day "A" Company's survey party made a reconnaissance of the division to avoid the viaduct near Le Cateau. By using a metre gauge line road bed prepared by the enemy from Honnechy to the sugar refinery, it would be possible to "Y" into the Le Cateau Yard, but the grade of 28 per cent was too much as it stood. A survey of the German yard in Honnechy west of the old French yard was also made. With the day's work, the main line between Busigny and Honnechy was opened for traffic. In Bohain Yard ballasting and work on the hospital siding were done. Advanced Battalion Headquarters began moving to a point near Busigny. At a conference among the Army Engineer Staff Officer and representatives, the 1st C.R.T., the French and Col. Clarke and Major Gibson at Busigny on the 26th, it was agreed that the Battalion carry on with several spurs along the line in conjunction with the French, while the 1st C.R.T. laid steel on the line from Busigny to Wassigny, excluding the later yard, whence the 2nd C.R.T. would carry on to Le Cateau.

Between St. Quentin and Busigny steel was complete, except for 2,500 feet to be laid by the French. The first train from the south reached Bohain at 1130 hours that day. In Bohain Yard switches were partly installed on the hospital siding and at Honnechy 300 feet of steel was taken from No. 3 and placed on No. 9 track, and five of the ten damaged enemy ammunition trucks were cleared from the line. Advanced Battalion Headquarters, located at a farm between Busigny and Maretz, was practically undamaged by war, and had room for all the animal transport in weathertight stables. By the following day the line from St. Quentin through Busigny was complete for single track. In Bohain Yard the debris of the bridge was cleared on the hospital spur and the latter completely ballasted. In Honnechy Yard the ambulance siding was converted. On the line between Wassigny and Le Cateau five brick bridges had been blown and on a high hill there was a crater. Only about a third of the steel could be used, as the enemy had systematically blown nearly all the joints. "A" Company moved a party of 40 all ranks from Busigny to the vicinity of Wassigny to work in the yard towards Le Cateau.

Following a complaint from the French that the bridge at Fonsomme was not safe, Major Gibson visited it the next morning, to find that in clearing the debris from the road below, the French had picked holes in the foundation to a depth in places of 18 inches, thus undermining the wall on which the bents were founded, and as it was checked, left it likely to fall unless prevented. The danger was increased when the French laid steel over it, for they joined two rails of different section, the joint with a difference in height of $3/8$-inch in the middle of the span, so that a train passing over it transmitted a very severe impact to the structure. This was remedied by replacing the rail with another of the same section, and to prevent further checking of the wall, a timber facing with a well-packed cinder backfill was built against it. It was arranged that "A" Company move to St. Benin and "C" to St. Souplet. On the line between Bohain and Busigny, the craters were 80 per cent filled for double track, but in Bohain Yard, although a mile and a half of sidings were ready for steel, it was impossible to do more since the steel had not arrived. In Busigny Yard more work was done on the hospital spur and on the craters. At Honnechy a party cleaned a well for supplying water to locomotives. With a German pump found in it and the aid of a French steam thresher, it was hoped to make a satisfactory plant. The "A" Company party began clearing and repairing the Wassigny Yards at the junction at the northwest end.

During the month on broad gauge lines 1.3 miles was located, 5.9 graded, 20.2 of grade repaired, 29.2 miles of track laid, 20 of track ballasted and 9.6 of track surfaced, while five railway bridges were built and 23 great mine craters were filled. The craters on the main Bohain-Busigny track were now filled 90 per cent complete for double track by the 29th. In Bohain Yard two switches were laid for the hospital spur and the spur into the sugar refinery, and old, damaged steel was stripped. On "C" Company moving to St. Souplet, "D" took over the entire yard. In Honnechy the work on the sidings and the water supply system continued. Labour used on the various jobs consisted of the 12th, 83rd and 90th Labour Companies, the 78th Burmese and 76th Chinese Labour Companies and the 6th Middlesex Labour Company. Prisoners of war were used in Bohain by "D" Company. On the Busigny-Le Cateau line the single track was completed to the bridge the following day; on the Wassigny-Le Cateau line steel and debris on the bridge near St. Benin were cleared, and on the bridge at Fassiaux the debris was a quarter cleared. At Busigny the ambulance and special stone spurs were opened for traffic. The unit was advised to pay special attention to mines on the line and to inspect everything carefully, as mines sometimes exploded several weeks after the withdrawal of the enemy.

On 1st November "A" Company was located at St. Benin, "B" at Le Cateau, "C" at St. Souplet, "D" at Bohain, the Maintenance Company at Montigny Farm and the Transport Company and Technical Stores with Headquarters at Busigny, with the same labour, but the 78th Burmese Labour Company was not working, as it claimed its year's contract had expired and that it should be sent home. On the Bohain-Busigny line "D" Company continued the work, while in Bohain Yard the remaining 1,200 feet was laid for the hospital siding by 0845 hours and the siding was ready to receive traffic. The stone siding was stripped ready for relaying the next day. Two small mines in the yard exploded, but the craters were quickly filled. Steel was laid in St. Souplet Yard, and debris was cleared at the bridge sites. At one of the latter the assistance of a tank from the 10th Tank Battalion was given. The tank was attached to the twisted steelwork of the fallen bridge and in a few months the work was accomplished. Debris was cleared from Le Cateau Yard, track was repaired there and steel was removed from the sidings. At Honnechy the pump was repaired and a start made on filling the 12,000 gallon tank. At night shelling was prevalent near the camps of "A" and "B" Companies.

Three more delayed mines exploded the following day in Bohain Yard while 600 feet of steel was being laid, but were soon repaired and traffic was resumed. In Wassigny Yard a mile of steel was removed and in St. Souplet Yard all the damaged steel was taken from one track and 850 yards laid on two others. At Le Cateau "B" Company began repairing the ramp in the yard and the sidings and clearing the bridge. The main line steel was now 75 per cent complete, and at Honnechy the water point was completed and some track in the yard repaired. The next day the delayed mines in Bohain Yard continued to explode, three under switches, which, however, were repaired in an hour as they were small. Another exploded on the hospital spur, but fortunately no train was on it, and the spur was opened by noon. On the stone spur there 600 feet was laid and the second track of the engineer's yard stripped preparatory to relaying. At the Wassigny end of the Wassigny-Le Cateau Yard the 83rd Labour Company removed 5,600 feet of damaged steel and replaced some 2,000 damaged ties. In St. Souplet Yard all the shell holes were filled and 1,000 yards of steel was laid, while the clearing of debris for placing the foundations of the bents on the bridge was 80 per cent complete, but there was no sign yet of the bridge timber. The work of repairing track in Le Cateau Yard continued. The train of Gen. Rawlinson, Commanding the Fourth Army, put in at the siding at Busigny that day, and the unit's technical stores train was brought down from Honnechy and placed in the factory siding.

In the early hours of the 4th, three more mines exploded in Bohain Yard and the bridge. The work of repair in conjunction with the French began, the unit parties taking the late shift on the bridge and working through the night building the two central piers. That day word was received of the signing of the armistice with Austria-Hungary. The switch of Bohain in the R.E. yard was completed and 2,000 feet of steel was laid. Reconstruction of the tracks in the yard at St. Souplet continued, 4,280 yards of damaged steel was removed to the south and 1,100 yards of new steel laid. The 83rd Labour Company removed steel from the line as far as Wassigny, while clearing debris from the bridges between St. Souplet and Le Cateau continued and a small party of "A" Company ballasted in Honnechy Yard. "B" Company's camp was severely shelled and Spr. T.L. Whale, a despatch rider, was killed and Spr. J. Dryton wounded, as were three other men of a tank corps staying in the camp overnight. The problem of mines was becoming serious, as ration trains were prevented from going farther forward than Fresnoy-le Grand, and as a result the rations were considerably reduced, although the unit was able to go to other dumps for an issue by means of its mechanical transport. It appeared that the enemy had been working on the preparation of mines since the previous June, giving particular attention to high fills, drifting in from the side and running longitudinal tunnels parallel to the line for placing the explosive charges.

Early the following morning a crater 40 yards across and 60 feet deep was blown by a mine about 1,500 feet south of Bohain Station on the line. Work on it began at once, but soon afterwards another mine of equal size exploded about 3,000 feet north of Bohain at a culvert, killing a prisoner of war and wounding three others. That day four other small mines exploded. In conjunction with the French, because all traffic was severed, "D" Company with a large party of prisoners of war tried to open the main line between Fresnoy-le Grand and Busigny. The ramp in Le Cateau yard was completed and work done on the bridge. On the other bridge the parties discovered several live shells and aerial torpedoes in the abutments ready for detonation, but they were removed before any harm was done. At St. Souplet the clearance of the bridge continued and steel was completed on a siding of the yard. In Honnechy Yard in response to instructions the metre gauge line was widened for use by the train of the General Officer Commanding. Spr. Whale was buried that afternoon in the British cemetery near Premont.

To ensure that traffic would not be interrupted by mines between Bohain and Fresnoy, work began the next day on a diversion, 2,000 feet being laid, but progress was slow as material had to be manhandled from Bohain Yard. Work on the recent mine craters was very heavy because of the continual rain, but for a change no mines went up that day after 17 in the unit sector to date. Work continued on all bridges and repairs were made to sidings in St. Souplet and Le Cateau Yards. The new siding at Honnechy completed, the train of Gen. Rawlinson moved on it. A careful inspection of the Wassigny-Le Cateau line revealed no mines. The 4,000-foot diversion from Bohain to avoid the mines section, on which worked 500 prisoners, was completed the ensuing morning. Another mine exploded at the road crossing at the end of the Bohain Yard and in the evening another under the switch from the hospital siding to the main line, closing the line for traffic between Fresnoy le Grand and Bohain. Several of the party working near the first mine escaped narrowly, but none was hurt.

The 90th Labour Company moved to St. Benin for attachment to "A" Company on the 8th, while "D" Company officers went to Wassigny to prepare a new camp. In the evening the lack of gun flashes in the sky was unusual, while throughout the day there had been rumours of the arrival of enemy envoys to receive terms of an armistice. Major Gibson went to Cambrai the following day to try to accelerate the shipment of bridging material to the Battalion. The delay was caused chiefly by the lack of locomotives there, so arrangements were made with the Railway Operating Department at Busigny to furnish the engine. The train of timber and sleepers was, therefore, expected the next day. The steel which should have accompanied the order was given to another unit, as it was urgently needed to build a spur for Field Marshal Haig's train in the Third

Army area. The steel was to be refunded to the 2nd C.R.T. the next day. The 21st and 714th Labour Companies were attached that day, the former going to "C" Company and the latter to work on the leg of the "Y" at Busigny. The work of repairs on the Wassigny-Le Cateau line continued, the bridge parties clearing debris and filling craters. The next day the big topic of conversation was the abdication of the Kaiser. The timber and other material for the Wassigny-Le Cateau line began arriving, so the framing of bents began. "D" Company moved by train to Wassigny to take over the work in the yard and the new "Y" with the 83rd Labour Company.

On the 11th, the diarist comments: "The best telegram ever received by this Battalion arrived today at 1115 hours. It read: 'To 2nd C.R.T. Day's date 11th. Hostilities cease 1100 hours today. From R.C.E.4'" In keeping with the news, the weather was bright and cheerful. Although the fighting had stopped, it was necessary for the unit to push on to extend its lines into the enemy's country to enable the Armies of Occupation to advance and bring them supplies. Timber was arriving satisfactorily by the 12th, and the unit hoped to have the line open by the 18th, although it would be necessary to use night shifts. Steel was laid northward from Wassigny and on the "Y" there grading was more than 90 per cent completed. On the bridges the parties were busy framing the bents, and on the craters two shifts were employed.

CHAPTER XV

THE CHARLEROI AREA

The unit was advised on 13th November that it would probably move well ahead when the Wassigny-Le Cateau line was built and continue reconstruction of the line towards Charleroi and Namur. Engaged in building a line from Honnechy to Le Cateau for the past week to avoid the fallen viaduct, the 7th C.R.T. was stopped that day, as their right of way ran through buildings and the French refused permission to demolish them. The chief news was that of the abdication of the kings of the German principalities. On the Wassigny "Y" steel was laid connecting the Le Cateau and Busigny lines, and steel was repaired north of St. Souplet. Plans showing location, type of change and date of explosion of mines on the railway lines in the neighbourhood were received the following day, so parties of the unit Maintenance Company helped remove them. Many were scheduled to explode towards the end of December but had already detonated, so the information was not considered overly reliable. For the most part they were sunk about 18 inches to two feet below the bed and consisted of shells and aerial torpedoes with acid cup detonators. German prisoners as well as men of the Battalion helped locate and remove them.

On the chord of the triangle near Busigny the next day, the 12th and 714th Labour Companies carried on the work of filling craters with the aid of scrapers and teams from the unit Transport Company. On the Wassigny "Y" steel was completed and ballasting began, while good progress was made on all bridges but one, where there was a shortage of material. Steel was made complete on the 16th from the Lassigny "Y" to the St. Souplet Bridge. Several of the Battalion went to Amiens to be interviewed by the Royal Air Force, but found that no more applications were being entertained. Steel was completed into the Le Cateau Yard the following day and laid over the bridge. Although the water supply system was only 85 per cent finished, it would be possible to furnish water the next day, if necessary. The parties on the Wassigny "Y" finished the ballasting, and "B" Company's bridge was completed. On the 18th the Wassigny-Le Cateau line was in operation as far as Le Cateau, the main work being finishing the bridges and sidings. In Le Cateau Yard the water system was ready for use and pumping began at 1630 hours. After two hours of pumping, it was found that there was still no water in the tank, so a search started for the leak, which was very difficult in the darkness, but eventually it was found at the other end of the yard. A new search then started to find the valve to cut that section, and after tracing the various pipe lines for some time the valve was located and the broken line isolated, after which pumping started in earnest. The French that day resurveyed the Busigny chord and altered the grade and the alignment.

The principal work the following day was on the sidings in Le Cateau and St. Souplet Yards, and in putting the final touches on the bridges. The widening of fills over craters continued on the main line and some lifting and ballasting was done. Surfacing was also carried out on the Wassigny "Y" and at St. Souplet Yards, and in putting the final touches on the bridges. At St. Souplet the work of clearing the wrecked German locomotive began. The train bearing the steel beams 47 feet long and the timber for the bridge at Le Cateau moved into the yard at 1430 hours, the first train there. Two of the eight standpipes in the yard were now operating. The next day Majors Gibson and Holdsworth went to look over the condition of the lines as far as Lobbes, near Charleroi, to find that between Le Cateau and that place the enemy had blown road crossings, bridges and other points as of old. They found a large quantity of bridge steel at Lobbes, including several girders 87 feet long. On the Wassigny-Le Cateau line general maintenance was done on the main line and yards and on the bridge at Le Cateau a steam crane raised the six girders. Preparations having been made during the morning, while the men were at lunch the lifting party raised the six in 30 minutes. The entire bridge, aside from clearing debris at the start, was rebuilt in one and a half hours. On the Wassigny "Y", widening of the fill and ballasting was carried on as well as removing the gantry in the yard. The old German locomotive in Le Cateau yard was removed and the track repaired. The unit was advised that short passes to places of interest might be granted, and to assist in this, the standing regulations as to the use of mechanical transport had been cancelled. As the diarist commented: "This means that joy-riding is now a legitimate pastime."

Signs of peace appearing daily included the lifting of censorship regulations far enough to permit giving the unit location and describing its surroundings in correspondence. The order prohibiting the use of cameras was also removed. Another order stated that no more commissions from the ranks would be approved until the surplus of officers at the Canadian Railway Troops Depot had been absorbed by units in the field. Now that the Wassigny-Le Cateau line was open for traffic, the work of the Battalion was chiefly maintenance on the main line and in the yards. The Busigny Chord was completed on the 21st, except at one spot where it was suspected there was still a mine. Capt. Muir succeeded Capt. Flood as adjutant. The Maintenance Company under Major Graham was disbanded on the 23rd. The personnel returned to their own companies, except for Lieut. Duckworth and six other ranks of "B", who were working with the 21st and 714th Labour Companies on the Busigny Chord. That day on removing a suspected mine, it was found to be a "dud", consisting of flying pigs and shells. The unit was advised the following day that to accelerate dental treatment the dental laboratory and personnel from the 9th C.R.T. would be sent to it. As the unit had been without dental facilities apart from those of the various Casualty Clearing Stations until August, the teeth of the men were in poor condition. Even after a dental officer arrived, it was difficult to treat the large number requiring plates, as all impressions had to be sent to the laboratories at Audricq or to the 6th C.R.T.

The unit began sending a lorry with four men from each company, three from transport, one from technical stores and machine shops and two from Battalion Headquarters for leave of 36 hours to Lille in charge of a Sergeant, while leave to England opened somewhat and in the past ten days the unit received four passes. Instructions were received to send a party to Ham-sur-Heure a few miles southwest of Charleroi to remove a blown German ammunition train in a tunnel there on the 25th, so Lieut. Draper and about 20 other ranks of "A" Company left by lorry the next day with tackle and tools and rations for several days. In the previous month the unit had located 1.8 miles, graded 4.42, repaired 21.36 miles of grade, laid 43.15 miles of track, ballasted 2.3 miles and surfaced 30 miles. "A" Company's detachment under Lieut. Draper at Jamiouix near Charleroi found that the train load of ammunition had been blown on the 16th and that the surrounding country looked as if a cyclone had passed. There must also have been a large casualty list of human beings and animals judging from the amount of charred equipment strewn about. The party was somewhat disconcerted by the explosion of a shell in the wreck caused by the still smouldering fire. Instructions came on the 30th to move this detachment at Jamiouix to the vicinity of Lobbes to remove the wrecks of two ammunition trains from the line to Charleroi.

On this date a summary of the total work performed by the unit in France revealed the fact that 61.85 miles of standard gauge track had been located, 57.19 graded, 76.11 miles of grade repaired, 154.9 miles of track laid, 85.8 miles ballasted, 75.55 miles surfaced, and 101.5 miles maintained. A total of 207.7 miles of narrow gauge lines had been located, 122.15 graded, 57.15 miles of grade repaired, 130.45 miles of track laid, 114.35 miles ballasted, 130.3 miles surfaced and 311.2 miles maintained.

On 1st December in the Charleroi area, Lieut. Draper went to Hourpes to enquire into preparations to clear the line of more burnt ammunition trains. The whole yard was a mass of fused ammunition, which would make the work difficult if not dangerous. The Belgian Chef-de-Gare said that the enemy blew the train the third day after the armistice was signed. The Railway Operating Department the following midnight took over the operation of the Wassigny-Le Cateau line, but the unit continued to operate the pump for the water supply. The Jamiouix party of "A" Company moved to Hourpes and began clearing the wreck there, after making arrangements with the Belgian authority at St. Martins for a locomotive to assist. The party was instructed the next day to unload nine agricultural engines from trucks, examine them and place them near the road.

Two Y.M.C.A. Canadian Railway Troops concert parties arrived at Busigny on the 5th, and one of them gave a performance the following evening by candlelight. As the performers had nothing but their costumes, a piano was obtained and blankets used as scenery and a drop curtain. The smaller party gave two concerts on Sunday, 8th December, at "D" Company's camp at Wassigny. That party was even worse off for props than the other, as the members did not even have costumes, but gave an excellent performance.

The demobilization scheme became a factor of primary interest to everyone. It appeared that length of service, married men first, was the main consideration, the occupational groupings being utilized only to facilitate the absorption of men as openings were afforded by the demand for various trades and callings. The service grouping divided the troops into 34 groups covering the period from the beginning of the war until 31st December, 1918. Groups 1 to 17 were married men or widowers with children, and 18 to 34 single men and widowers without children. Designated by the letters "A" to "U", 21 dispersal centres in Canada ran from "A" in Prince Edward Island to "U" at Victoria, B.C. An individual could choose any centre, irrespective of place of enlistment.

The unit was advised on the 10th that more work lay at Fontaine-Valmont, where the enemy destroyed a bridge 197¾ feet long over the Sambre River, as well as the track on each side of it. The French wished to rebuild this themselves, but to get the line open were willing for the British to build a diversion with a temporary bridge over the river. There was a fair supply of timber nearby in a small forest and in dumps. Orders were, therefore, issued for the movement forward of "A", "B" and "D" Companies to move the following day, followed by the other two companies, leaving "C" to take over all maintenance on the Wassigny-Le Cateau line. "B" Company went into comfortable billets at Fontaine-Valmont, where the Burgomaster was full of regrets at his inability to supply beds for everyone. Grading of the diversion started on the 14th on the western approach to the site of the bridge over the Sambre. That day the unit received a request for coal miners, qualified and willing to work in the Nova Scotia mines. Most of "D" Company moved to Fontaine-Valmont the next day, when word was received that a steam pile driver was being sent there. The Battalion was instructed to send up to 50 "B" Category and other specially qualified men for early return to Canada in parties of not more than 20 to the Canadian General Base, Etaples. This was followed by a request for bakers and butchers for duty in Concentration Wings in England.

At Fontaine-Valmont grading continued on the diversion and a foot bridge over the Sambre was completed on the 17th, but the work was hindered by rain. Eight waggon loads of timber were cut in the forest the next day and a train load of material was received from Lobbes. The 35th Labour Company started work there that day. Two timber lorries were sent by the 4th C.R.T. to assist in moving salvaged timbers, and on the 20th a steam lorry was used to haul the timber from Marpent to the bridge. The unit was assigned the task of building a temporary bridge at Jeumont in this area. Half of "A" Company moved to La Buissière near Fontaine Valmont on the 21st.

More definite news arrived as to the future with the information that after the next day each C.R.T. Battalion which could be relieved would go to Etaples and that after the New Year all would be relieved and moved as accommodation was available. It was hoped to have them all out of France by the end of January. On reaching Etaples, the Battalion would be broken up and sent to the Regimental Depot in drafts as transportation became available. On arrival at the Depot, each unit would reassemble, be disbanded into service groups and sent to the Concentration Camp for return to Canada.

Christmas was merry, at La Buissière the people showing great readiness to help the men. A large hall, electrically lighted, was secured and tables were built. On Christmas Day at Busigny Battalion Headquarters dined in one of the numerous buildings on the farm. The menu consisted of soup, roast turkey, mashed potatoes, peas, plum pudding and apricot pie, besides nuts, apples, oranges, cigarettes and coffee. At Fontaine-Valmont, the non-commissioned officers served the men, after which the latter gave an impromptu concert. At St. Souplet Officers and Sergeants served the men of "C" Company, and at La Buissière the Transport Company had its dinner first and then "A" Company. That year the people of Manitoba provided plum pudding for everyone, and all who came from Ontario received a box from the Government of that province. From the Ladies' Auxiliary of the 127th Battalion came a liberal gift of cigarettes and tobacco.

In common with the remainder of the infantry of the Non-Permanent Active Militia after the war, the 12th Regiment, York Rangers, dropped its number, becoming known as "The York Rangers", but like the Queen's Own Rifles of Canada and the Royal Highlanders of Canada, on reorganization it was authorized to maintain two battalions, the 1st Battalion a county and the 2nd a city unit, under the command of (on promotion) Col. Clarke [1]. Among the officers of the 1st Battalion who had served in France with the 127th Battalion, C.E.F. (2nd Battalion, Canadian Railway Troops) were Major J. M. Gibson, D.S.O., Major G. B. Little, Major A. H. S. Adams, Capts. J. M. Muir, H. W. B. Smith, L. F. Johnston, A. R. Clarke and J. C. Boylen, the latter as paymaster, Lt.-Col. R. M. Hillary, V.D., as senior medical officer, and Hon. Capt. T. G. McGonigle, the chaplain. With the 2nd Battalion those who had served with the 2nd C.R.T. included Major J. H. Craig and Capt. W. R. Smith.

---

[1] 7th January, 1922.

APPENDIX "A"

Officers of the 127th Battalion, C.E.F.
(On Embarkation from Canada, 21-8-1916)

Lt.-Col.	CLARKE, Frederick Fieldhouse
Major	AGNEW, John
Major	CAMPBELL, Harry Cheshel
Major	HILLARY, Robert Michael
Major	HOLDSWORTH, Thomas Henry
Capt.	ADAMS, Andrew Hepburn S.
Capt.	BELL, John Renwick
Capt.	BOYLEN, John Chancellor
Capt.	CRAIG, James Henry
Capt.	FLOOD, Albert James
Capt.	GIBSON, John McIntyre
Capt.	JOHNSTON, Edwin Lavergne
Capt.	LAWRENCE, Allen Russell
Capt.	McGONIGLE, Thomas George
Capt.	MUIR, James Murray
Lieut.	ANDERSON, Hugh Caldwell
Lieut.	BRUNTON, Reginald Ruston * (M.C. with 75 Bn., C.E.F.)
Lieut.	CAMERON, Alexander Osborn L.
Lieut.	CLARKE, Albert Ross
Lieut.	DRAPER, Henry Charles
Lieut.	JENKINS, James Thomas
Lieut.	JOHNSTON, Lyman Ferguson
Lieut.	KNOX, John Henry
Lieut.	LITTLE, George Burnfield
Lieut.	McILWRAITH, Alexander Hamilton
Lieut.	McINTOSH, Peter Douglas
Lieut.	MAGEE, Harold William
Lieut.	RITCHIE, George Frederick
Lieut.	SMITH, Harry Batoche W.
Lieut.	SMITH, William Ryrie
Lieut.	VAN NORMAN, Clarence Percival
Lieut.	WALLACE, James Hugh G.

* Killed in Action, Passchendaele, 31st October, 1917.

APPENDIX "B"

The Roll of Honour
2nd Battalion, Canadian Railway Troops
(127th Battalion, C.E.F.)

1917

Capt.		Hugh Caldwell ANDERSON	D.W. 11-8-17
Major		Thomas Ninian ELLIOTT	K.A. 28-9-17
Hon. Capt.		Edwin Levergne JOHNSTON	D. (Can.) 10-11-17
733338	Spr.	BALSMAN, S. C.	D. 7-9-17
410025	Spr.	BIGRAS, A. A.	D.W. 29-7-17
208312	Spr.	BOUCHARD, W.	D.W. 11-11-17
778419	Spr.	CHAPMAN, R.	K.A. 4-9-17
195043	Spr.	COONES, H.	D. 16-3-17
778391	Spr.	DILLON, D. J.	D.W. 3-7-17
805547	Spr.	FARR, P. F.	D.W. 7-6-17
778108	Spr.	GREENBURY, C. M.	K.A. 3-10-17
778085	Spr.	HARRIS, W.	D.W. 21-4-17
1081351	Cpl.	HYETT, W. J.	K.A. 8-11-17
778604	Cpl.	LEARMOUTH, J. C.	D.W. 12-7-17
625156	Spr.	McINTOSH, J. W.	K.A. 2-8-17
1081971	Spr.	RUDDIMAN, W.	D.Inj. 4-2-17
778562	Cpl.	RUSHWORTH, J.	K.A. 2-7-17
778626	Spr.	SHAWCROSS, J. H.	K.A. 25-6-17
1082194	Spr.	SIEGEL, H.	D.W. 8-11-17
778242	Spr.	SWINGLER, H.	D.W. 25-6-17
778847	Spr.	TAIT, W. G.	D.W. 25-6-17
675281	Spr.	THOMAS, J. H.	D.W. (Acc.) 17-5-17
164229	Spr.	TURNER, R.	D.W. 18-9-17
733195	Spr.	WALSH, E. C.	D.W. 12-7-17
4903	Sgt.	WALKEY, W.J. (C.A.S.C.)	D.W. 12-7-17

1918

Lieut.		John Henry KNOX	K.A. 30-3-18
225524	Spr.	BAKER, G. A.	D. 20-12-18
1078639	Spr.	DALEY, F., M.M.	D. 20-12-18
778809	Cpl.	DAY, G. E., M.M.	D. 9-5-18

218447	Spr.	DUNCAN, B.	D. 20-2-18
2502959	Spr.	FAVELLE, A. T. J.	M.P.D. 30-3-18
512791	Spr.	GREGAN, J. J.	D. 14-9-18
778609	Spr.	GRIFFITHS, E.	K.A. 30-3-18
200931	Spr.	LAMB, W. F.	D. 18-12-18
1081780	Spr.	LONG, B. S.	D. 18-12-18
778132	Sgt.	MacKENZIE, D. R.	D.W. 30-3-18
778316	Spr.	MAGEE, J.	D. 2-12-18
778456	Spr.	MORLAND, D.	D. (Can.) 4-9-18
778400	Spr.	MORRISON, J. W.	K.A. 17-2-18
925817	Spr.	PARBERY, J. H.	D. 20-12-18
733775	Spr.	SIBLEY, R. E.	D. 8-11-18
778355	Spr.	STOOT, C. L. V.	D. 3-12-18
778563	Spr.	TULLY, N. J.	D. Inj. 8-1-18
865257	Spr.	VINCENT, J. M.	D. 26-11-18
778385	Spr.	WHALE, T. L.	K.A. 4-11-18
778348	Cpl.	WHIRTAM, E.	D. (Can.) 30-10-18

1919

3080485	Spr.	BLACKWOOD, J.	D. 23-1-19
778886	Spr.	COLE, P. E.	D. (U.K.) 7-2-19
778436	R.Q.M.S.	GRAHAM, T. R., M.S.M.	D. (U.K.) 9-2-19
761124	Spr.	HOOPER, F. J.	K. (Acc.) 1-1-19
779073	L/Cpl.	McELDON, A. J.	D. (U.K.) 30-1-19
905146	Spr.	MELESHKO, S.	D. (U.K.) 28-1-19
779034	Spr.	PARKER, R. C.	D. (Can.) 15-10-19
779043	Spr.	ROSS, G. G.	D. 31-1-19
778351	Sgt.	SCOTT, J., M.M.	D. 22-1-19
778952	Spr.	SMITH, J. J.	D. (Can.) 7-5-19
2497683	Spr.	STOKES, E.	D. 21-1-19
1081006	Spr.	VALENTINE, W.	D. (U.K.) 1-3-19

1920

2499578	Spr.	BEAULIEU, R. A.	D. 24-3-20
1075276	Cpl.	CAMPBELL, N. P.	D. 12-2-20
3030603	Spr.	IVANOSKI, A.	D. 15-1-20
219406	Spr.	LANGLOIS, L.	D. 31-3-20
2204779	Spr.	LAW, R. F.	D. 17-5-20
111311	Spr.	MacLEOD, K. H.	D. 6-12-20
675098	Spr.	THOMAS, A. E.	D. 15-7-20

1922

405752	Spr.	FOX, W.	D. 5-4-22
778918	Spr.	VERNON, G. E.	D. 20-1-22

K.A.	— Killed in Action
K.	— Killed
D.	— Died
D.W.	— Died of Wounds
M.P.D.	— Missing, Presumed Dead
D. Inj.	— Died of Injuries

APPENDIX "C"

A partial list of non-fatal casualties

515284	Dvr.	FLYNN, H. C.	13- 4-17
651037	Spr.	NICHOLSON, N.	14- 4-17
778356	Spr.	WAGSTAFF, H. R.	16- 4-17
778085	Spr.	*HARRIS, W.	18- 4-17
778071	Spr.	WESTBEARE, W. H.	18- 4-17
778497	Cpl.	CAMPBELL, L. D. V.	23- 4-17
778488	Spr.	SHEPPARD, W. J.	10- 5-17
857573	Spr.	PREVENCHER, A.	24- 5-17
318115	Spr.	LLEWELLYN, I. S.	7- 6-17
778166	Spr.	GIBSON, F.	7- 6-17
898106	Spr.	WALKER, H. M.	7- 6-17
285201	Spr.	SKELLY, J.	7- 6-17
339064	Spr.	MANSON, W.	7- 6-17
778341	Spr.	YEOMANS, G. H.	8- 6-17
778900	Spr.	McVEY, J. A.	8- 6-17
835907	Spr.	DAY, W.	16- 6-17
778635	Cpl.	REID, J. H.	12- 6-17
928916	Spr.	TAYLOR, J.	12- 6-17
779083	Spr.	COOPER, F.	12- 6-17
778366	Cpl.	BOUVAIR, T. H.	13- 6-17
743031	Spr.	BOONE, D.	12- 6-17
171568	Cpl.	HICKS, C. H.	20- 6-17
778582	L/Cpl.	RAYNSFORD, R.	20- 6-17
778994	Spr.	THOMPSON, D.S.	24- 6-17

* Died 21-4-17

715483	Spr.	ROSS, E.H.	24- 6-17
778323	Cpl.	BARTON, A. T.	24- 6-17
	Lieut.	A. G. BONN	25- 6-17
778184	Sgt.	MARTIN, G.	25- 6-17
778332	Spr.	HARDING, W. J.	25- 6-17
1075316	Spr.	VITMER, J. F.	25- 6-17
687374	Spr.	DREW, B. E.	25- 6-17
743118	Spr.	ELLIS, F.	25- 6-17
778407	Spr.	WATSON, O.	27- 6-17
778689	Spr.	GRUNDY, E.	2- 7-17
163219	Spr.	TYTLER, A. A.	2- 7-17
805110	Spr.	DOWIE, W.	2- 7-17
734261	Spr.	STODDART, E.	2- 7-17
195892	Spr.	ALLEN, P.	2- 7-17
805110	Spr.	McCONNELL, T.	2- 7-17
742012	Spr.	LOGAN, J. P.	2- 7-17
823583	Spr.	KARSWILL, C. M.	6- 7-17
415366	Spr.	BOWRON, C. A.	6- 7-17
733195	Spr.	† WALSH, E. C.	9- 7-17
	Lt.	A. R. CLARKE	10- 7-17
	Lt.	L. F. JOHNSTON	12- 7-17
1082191	Spr.	WHALBERG, W.	14- 7-17
779051	Spr.	CAMPBELL, N. E.	16- 7-17
778498	Spr.	BOYS, H. W.	19- 7-17
636819	Spr.	FITZGERALD, G. A.	20- 7-17
742414	Spr.	SKINNER, R. M.	23- 7-17
733257	Spr.	WOLFE, S. I.	23- 7-17
898523	L/Cpl.	FORTIER, A. L.	26- 7-17
778996	Spr.	ROBERTSON, E. A.	26- 7-17
895218	Spr.	FORTH, H. G.	29- 7-17
1081385	Spr.	KRUYFF, J.	29- 7-17
787338	Spr.	SMITH, W. B.	28- 7-17
	Lt.	H. C. DRAPER	28- 7-17
778313	Cpl.	ROSS, G. R.	30- 7-17
778343	Spr.	MEARS, R. G.	1- 8-17
778579	Spr.	RICHARDSON, H. S.	1- 8-17

† Died of Wounds 12-7-17

778507	Spr.	MAY, W.	4- 8-17
778827	Spr.	WATTS, T. H.	6- 8-17
778426	Spr.	ARCHER, H. F.	6- 8-17
856677	Spr.	RASSI, D.	8- 8-17
901755	Spr.	MALONEY, J. J.	12- 8-17
778845	Spr.	CLARK, H.	16- 8-17
778051	Cpl.	HILL, S.	12- 8-17
778348	Cpl.	WHITTAM, E.	18- 8-17
725160	Cpl.	DEMPSTER, J.	10- 8-17
733987	Spr.	MacPHEE, R. B.	10- 8-17
761267	Spr.	HUSSELTON, E.	10- 8-17
207704	Spr.	HANSEN, J.	18- 8-17
207689	Spr.	ROBERTS, A.	23- 8-17
779041	Spr.	WHITTAM, J.	18- 8-17
928066	Spr.	YEATES, F.	21- 8-17
1075011	Spr.	SYMINGTON, A.	17- 9-17
733684	Spr.	CROUSE, S. C.	18- 8-17
733597	Spr.	WOODSWORTH, G. R.	15- 8-17
733090	Spr.	HOYT, H.	18- 8-17
835288	Spr.	ELLIOTT, J. W.	15- 8-17
195705	Spr.	RATCHFORD, P.	15- 8-17
1075255	Cpl.	FISHER, J.	10- 8-17
778975	Spr.	FISHER, L.	11- 8-17
1081122	Spr.	ELLIS, G. A.	11- 8-17
1081535	Spr.	LASHMAN, P.	7- 8-17
1081158	Spr.	MOCKFORD, W.	12- 8-17
406421	Spr.	WALLACE, W. G.	17- 8-17
778856	Spr.	WARD, T.	18- 8-17
1081910	Spr.	BURTON, G. E.	8- 8-17
114263	Spr.	BINGHAM, J.	19- 8-17
688200	Spr.	THOMPSON, G. L.	19- 8-17
778153	Spr.	VANDERBURGH, W. A.	22- 8-17
408753	Spr.	BLAIR, E. B.	25- 8-17
208020	Spr.	BURLIE, G. E.	6- 8-17
1081335	Spr.	CAPPUS, J. S.	1- 9-17
207199	A/L/Cpl.	MURPHY, K.	21- 9-17
637109	Spr.	WAY, E. A.	22- 9-17
778161	Sgt.	RAE, R. B.	22- 9-17
111311	Spr.	MacLEOD, K.	24- 9-17
733838	Spr.	WHITMAN, R. C.	27- 9-17
505476	Spr.	HECKBERT, W. R.	1-10-17
432031	Spr.	ASHTON, B.	22- 9-17
503771	A/L/Sgt.	OFFERDAHL, C.	1-10-17

733732	Spr.	MANSFIELD, L. S.	3-10-17
339865	Spr.	FRASER, P. G.	3-10-17
778325	Spr.	LEITCH, W.	10-10-17
	Lt.	G. E. THOMAS	11-10-17
2497465	Spr.	LAVIGNE, C.	13-10-17
216877	Spr.	McILROY, W. S.	15-10-17
778341	Spr.	YEOMANS, G. H.	17-10-17
779013	Spr.	FENWICK, L.	19-10-17
790112	L/Cpl.	BURRELL, P. L.	20-10-17
778493	Spr.	PETT, A. J.	21-10-17
778619	Spr.	WILLIAMS, T.	22-10-17
778373	Spr.	MAHER, J.	22-10-17
925714	Spr.	POOL, W. C.	22-10-17
279493	Spr.	COGGINS, T. E.	3-11-17
1081229	Spr.	INGER, E.	3-11-17
348632	Spr.	McRAE, G. L. B.	5-11-17
1039471	Spr.	McLEOD, K. T.	6-11-17
633685	Spr.	MALERTE, L.	6-11-17
1082194	Spr.	SIEGER, H.	8-11-17
651070	Spr.	DAVIES, F. W.	10-11-17
207162	Spr.	WILLIAMSON, J.	11-11-17
778785	Cpl.	PAGE, A.	11-11-17
778585	Spr.	KEWELL, J.	11-11-17
811984	Dvr.	McLEOD, J. K. (CASC)	11-11-17
2410	Sgt.	SHARP, J. A. (CASC)	11-11-17
742515	Spr.	HARDING, P. J.	12-11-17
1075245	Spr.	TAIT, J.	15-11-17
186739	Spr.	WOODHEAD, G. B.	15-11-17
1081085	Spr.	CADE, G.	19-11-17
733689	Spr.	CLATTENBURG, R.	20-11-17
734418	Spr.	DAVIS, W. E. T.	20-11-17
754382	Spr.	MATTHEWS, W.	20-11-17
438495	Spr.	NASE, W. E.	20-11-17
904940	Spr.	STEINHAVER, M. E.	20-11-17
1061939	Spr.	LATIMER, J.	22-11-17
761274	Spr.	GRAHAM, H.	6- 1-18
1007039	Spr.	FRASER, J.	6- 1-18
229543	Spr.	ALEY, H.	16- 2-18
778466	Cpl.	RIDING, E.	17- 2-18
115456	Cpl.	EASTWOOD, H.	17- 2-18
2497393	Spr.	GRAY, E. T.	17- 2-18
730297	Cpl.	PODGER, G. V.	26- 3-18

	Lt.	J. McA. SHARP	30- 3-18
669368	Spr.	SARGEANT, C. R.	24- 3-18
234293	A/L/Cpl.	CURTIS, H.	28- 3-18
651240	Spr.	ERNEST, E. F.	29- 3-18
778070	Spr.	BROOKS, C. G.	30- 3-18
779076	Spr.	DOUGLAS, W. G.	30- 3-18
928066	Spr.	YEATES, F.	30- 3-18
778132	Sgt.	MacKENZIE, D. R.	30- 3-18
742867	Spr.	GIBERTSON, H. E.	30- 3-18
679061	Spr.	BOYD, J. T.	30- 3-18
2502959	Spr.	FAVELLE, A. J. T.	30- 3-18
742986	A/L/Cpl.	BROWN, A.	30- 3-18
1081488	Spr.	LINSKY, J.	30- 3-18
778191	Cpl.	McGONIGLE, R. H.	30- 3-18
778058	Spr.	ORTON, G. A.	30- 3-18
432557	Spr.	SMITH, W.	30- 3-18
778071	Spr.	WESTBEARE, W. A.	30- 3-18
687522	Spr.	WILLS, A.	30- 3-18
760937	Spr.	SHAW, N.	30- 3-18
847848	Spr.	GAGNON, A.	30- 3-18
778366	Cpl.	BOVAIR, T. H.	30- 3-18
491289	Cpl.	FINNEY, A.	30- 3-18
2184431	Spr.	COYNE, N. E.	30- 3-18
734343	Spr.	WILSON, F.	30- 3-18
348632	Spr.	McREA, O. J. S.	30- 3-18
751451	Spr.	SCHNURR, J. W.	30- 3-18
285121	Spr.	COOLE, H. J.	30- 3-18
2184424	Spr.	ROOS, A.	30- 3-18
778747	Sgt.	TACK, H.	24- 9-18
734028	Spr.	CANNING, W. V.	25- 9-18
778308	Cpl.	LLOYD, R. M. (Acc.)	6-10-18
2503012	Spr.	DRYTON, J.	4-11-18

NOTE: Records of non-fatal casualties of the C.E.F. no longer exist, so this list was prepared chiefly from Battalion war diaries, all particulars lacking being inserted from other sources.

APPENDIX "D"

Honours and Awards			London Gazette Date
778327	Cpl.	BANKS, R.	M.M.	29- 8-18
105507	Spr.	BOGART, J. L. C.	M.M.	12- 6-18
	Lt.	BONN, A. G.	M.C.	22- 6-18
778996	Sgt.	CALDER, D.	M.S.M.	3- 6-19
	Lt.	CAMERON, A. O. L.	M.C.	18-10-17
			D.S.O.	1- 1-18
	Lt.-Col.	CLARKE, F. F.	Bar to D.S.O.	26- 7-18
			M. in D.	28-12-17
			M. in D.	31-12-18
			M.B.E., C.G. 27	6- 7-46
	Lt.	CLARKE, T. W.	M.C.	26-11-17
	Lt. (A/Capt.)	CLARKE, T. W.	M.B.E.	3- 6-19
	C.S.M.	COOPER, W. G. M.	M.S.M.	18- 1-19
778022	Spr.	DALEY, F.	M.M.	12- 6-18
1078639	Cpl.	DAY, G. E.	M.M. (Died 9-5-18)	28- 9-17
778809	Spr.	DE LUCIA, M.	M.M.	12- 6-18
2502816	Spr.	DOUGLAS, J. G.	M.M.	12- 6-18
779076	Cpl.	DUGGAN, J. J.	M.M.	29- 3-18
778826	Spr.	FENWICK, L.	M.M.	12-12-17
779013	Capt.	GALBRAITH, R. D.	M.C.	22- 6-18
	Major	GIBSON, J. McI.	M. in D.	31-12-18
			D.S.O.	3- 6-19
			M. in D.	11- 7-19
778256	Cpl.	GLOVER, J. L.	M.M.	12- 6-18
778069	Sgt.	GOULDING, J.	D.C.M.	1- 1-18
778436	RQM Sgt.	GRAHAM, T. R.	M.S.M.	3- 6-19
778051	Cpl. (A/Sgt.)	HILL, S.	M.M.	12- 6-18

778548	Major	HOLDSWORTH, T. H.	M. in D.	11- 7-19
778119	RQMS	INGROUILLE, T. J.	M.S.M.	3- 6-19
778091	Pte. (A/Cpl.)	JOYCE, J. A.	M.M.	19-11-17
784215	Cpl.	KENNEDY, C.	M.S.M.	1- 1-18
778440	Cpl.	KILLEN, R. J.	M.M.	12- 6-18
658017	Sgt.	KING, D.	M.S.M.	1- 1-18
778373	Cpl. (Spr.)	LENGARD, T. E.	M. in D.	28-12-17
778507	Spr.	MAHER, J. J.	M.M.	2- 4-18
760782	Sgt.	MAY, W.	M.M.	12- 6-18
348632	Cpl.	MILLS, M.	M.S.M.	17- 6-18
778554	Spr.	McRAE, O. L. S.	M.M.	17- 2-17
503771	Sgt.	NASH, J.	M.S.M.	3- 6-19
778140	Spr. (A/Cpl.)	OFFERDAHL, C.	M.M.	12-12-17
814622	Sgt.	RICHARDS, R. E.	M. in D.	28-12-17
	Sgt.	RICHARDS, W. F.	M.M.	29- 8-18
	Lt.	RITCHIE, G. F.	M. in D.	28- 5-18
778313	Cpl.	ROSS, G. R.	M. in D.	28-12-17
778225	Cpl. (L/Sgt.)	SAIGLE, E. G.	M.M.	12- 8-18
778351	Sgt.	SCOTT, J.	M.M.	29- 8-18
778745	Spr.	SMITH, F. S.	M.M.	12- 6-18
778124	Sgt.	SMITHERS, A.	M.M.	29- 8-18
			M.M.	28- 5-18
	Major	SWAN, W. G.	⎧ M. in D. ⎨ French Croix de Guerre ⎩ M. in D. D.S.O. O.B.E., C.G.I.	6-11-18 31-12-18 1- 1-19 6- 1-45
778205	Sgt.	WALTON, A. M.	M.M.	20- 8-19

APPENDIX "E"

SOME CITATIONS

Lieut Albert Guido Bonn, M.C.

For conspicuous gallantry and devotion to duty. When the enemy penetrated our line, he rallied his men and led them forward again to the original line, which despite the intense shell and machine gun fire, the company maintained although both its flanks were exposed. When the order to withdraw had been given, he assisted in carrying away a wounded N.C.O. under extremely heavy fire. His marked courage and gallantry and his untiring devotion to duty contributed greatly in holding up the enemy's advance.
—L.G. 30761, 22 Jun. 18.

Lieut. Alexander Osborn Lochiel Cameron, M.C.

For conspicuous gallantry and devotion to duty in maintaining light railway lines under heavy shell fire. He continually relaid the tracks under heavy shell fire, and kept them repaired and in working order throughout the operations. He set an excellent example of devotion to duty to his men. —L.G. 38561, 7 Mar. 18.

Lieut. Col. Frederick Fieldhouse Clarke, D.S.O.
(Bar to D.S.O.)

(Bar to D.S.O.) For conspicuous gallantry and devotion to duty during a hostile attack lasting for four days. He organized from his battalion sixteen Lewis gun teams, and made all arrangements for ammunition and supplies to be brought up to the front line by his own lorries. Except for the higher direction of the defence, the unit was entirely self-contained. The promptitude and alacrity with which this unit responded for volunteers, the splendid manner with which the defence was organized, the coolness and sustained enthusiasm displayed by all ranks under his command, were largely due to the courage, inspiring example and fine leadership of the Commanding Officer.
— L.G. 30813, 26 Jul. 18.

Mention in despatches. — L.G. 31089, 31 Dec. 18.
M.B.E. — C.G. 27, 6 Jul. 46.

Lieut. Thomas Walter Clarke, M.C.

For conspicuous gallantry and devotion to duty. When an ammunition dump caught fire he organized a party, and succeeded in extinguishing the fire before serious damage was done. He showed the greatest coolness and courage on this and many other occasions. —L.G. 30614, 6 Apr. 18.

Captain R. Douglas Galbraith, M.C.

For conspicuous gallantry and devotion to duty. Finding that the troops of other units on his right flank had withdrawn, he brought his company out in good order to a support trench 50 yards in rear. Going forward himself with a machine gun to his old position, he inflicted very heavy casualties on the enemy. Having expended all the available ammunition, he withdrew his men again to a comparatively sheltered position, where he reorganized and reinforced his company with men of other units. He then led his company forward to his first position, and maintained it until relieved. His personal example, great courage and devotion to duty had a most inspiring effect on all ranks.
—L.G. 30761, 22nd June, 1918.

Sergeant J. Goulding, D.C.M.

For conspicuous gallantry and devotion to duty. On one occasion, altough he and his party were three times shelled off the work, by his courage, coolness and skill, he completed it under heavy fire, thereby enabling a Naval gun to be put into the required position. —L.G. 30450, 17 Apr. 18.

APPENDIX "F"

DUTIES OF OFFICERS
2nd BATTALION, CANADIAN RAILWAY TROOPS

Engineering Headquarters Duties

Major J. M. Gibson, Chief Engineer

In charge of all Railway work under the direction of the Commanding Officer. Reports of works, material, supplies and locations and plans and allotment of labor.

Lieut. E. A. Ternan, Mechanical Engineer
In charge of repairs, water supplies and any other special duties assigned to him by the Commanding Officer.

Lieut.   Ass't. Chief Engineer Officer
For location and inspection purposes.

Lieut. J. E. Stark, Off. i/c Technical Stores
Officer in charge of material, yard, Technical and Engineering Stores, fuel for engines, etc.

Lieut. A. H. McIlwraith, Operating Officer
Operating Officer, i/c rolling stock on construction.

Administrative Department Duties

Major T. H. Holdsworth, 2nd in Command
In charge of Interior Economy and Discipline under the direction of the Commanding Officer.

Capt. A. J. Flood, Adjutant
In charge of all returns and states, Officers and N.C.O's. records and files, and correspondence from the O.C. and 2nd in Command of Administrative matter, and that all correspondence pertaining to Engineering be passed to the Chief Engineer.

Hon. Capt. E. L. Johnston, Quartermaster
In charge of all Camp and Barrack equipment issued to the Battalion from Ordnance and Barrack Stores. Will also arrange for the issue of clothing, rations, forage, fuel and oil to Battalion Headquarters and Companies, and all equipment according to Mobilization Store Table to be drawn through this Department.

Lieut. L. F. Johnston, Transport Officer
In charge of all Battalion Animals and Motor Transport, and the allotment of the same on requisition from the Officers i/c of the different departments. He will supervise log books and roster of the transport of Battalion Head-

quarters and the Companies, and is also responsible for the feeding of animals, and condition of stables. He will report to the V.O. at once of any animals that are sick and have them removed to the sick lines. He will make frequent inspection of stable picquet, and the state of equipment of animals, etc.

Attached

Major R. M. Hillary, Medical Officer

He will perform his duties as per the instruction of the D.M.S. In charge of all matters pertaining to the health of the men of the Battalion and attached units and will make frequent inspections of Camp and kitchens and report any irregularities.

Capt. J. J. O'Gorman, Veterinary Officer

He will perform his duties as per the instructions of the D.V.S. In charge of all matters pertaining to the health of the animals of the Battalion and attached units, and will make frequent inspections of stable and forage, and report any irregularities and is also permitted to arrange sick lines for treatment of animals at Battalion Headquarters.

Capt. J. C. Boylen, Paymaster and Ass't. Adjutant

"A" Branch

In charge of all Pay and Allowance claims Part II Orders and records and also compile War Diary. Headquarters Officers and O.C. Companies will forward their reports to him each Saturday for this purpose.

Stable Picquet

Duties will include the Blacksmith Shop and all transport, in addition to mules and horse stable.

Sanitary Police

Are under the Medical Officer and will maintain a diligent endeavor to keep the lines and quarters clean, reporting any irregularities.

Water Details

Attached to Companies for work under instruction of Medical Officer.

Military Police
Are under the Adjutant, will maintain order, discipline, and keep out unauthorized persons from quarters, work, stores, and yards of the Battalion. No person unless with permission will be allowed in above-mentioned places.

Fire Protection
Under Capt. A.J. Flood, Adjutant. All huts will keep two tins of clean water ready at all times in case of fire. A gasoline tin open at top can be used for this purpose. In case of fire the senior man, N.C.O. or an Officer takes charge, according to the situation. All employed men on Headquarters, Paymaster's, Quartermaster's and Medical Officer's Offices will act as the fire protection for Camp. The gong at Battalion Headquarters will ring in case of fire, when all men will go to allotted stations as per the Adjutant's instructions. All Companies attached to Headquarters will act under these instructions. Companies detached will provide their own fire protection.

APPENDIX "G"

Some of the Units attached to the 2nd C.R.T. as Labour (in Order of Attachment)

1917

Northumberland Fusiliers
East Surrey Regiment
7th Cheshire Regiment
12th York and Lancaster Regiment
6th Royal Berkshire Regiment (Princess Charlotte of Wales's)
Northamptonshire Regiment
7th Buffs (East Kent Regiment)
Royal Marine Light Infantry
13th York and Lancaster Regiment
Royal Naval Division: Drakes, Nelsons, Hawkes, Hoods
174th Tunnelling Company, R.E.
Duke of Cornwall's Light Infantry
Royal Sussex Regiment Pioneers
Royal Irish Fusiliers (Princess Victoria's)
Oxfordshire and Buckinghamshire Light Infantry

Royal Fusiliers (City of London Regiment)
2nd Queen's Royal Regiment (West Surrey)
4th Bedfordshire and Hertfordshire Regiment
11th Manchester Regiment
18th Labour Company
Suffolk Regiment
12th Battalion, York and Lancaster Regiment
9th West Yorkshire Regiment (The Prince of Wales's Own)
2nd Devonshire Regiment
20th Cheshire Regiment (Labour)
2nd/5th Duke of Wellington's Regiment (West Riding)
2nd/5th King's Own Yorkshire Light Infantry
2nd/5th York and Lancaster Regiment
187th Trench Mortar Battery
2nd/4th Duke of Wellington's Regiment (West Riding)
47th Battalion, Australians
48th Battalion, Australians
8th Battalion, Australians
29th Company, Royal Engineers
30th Battalion, Australians
20th Cheshire Regiment
29th Light Railway Operating Company, R.E.
53rd Battalion, Australians
58th Battalion, Australians
22nd West Yorkshire Regiment (The Prince of Wales's Own) (Labour)
12th South Staffordshire Regiment (Labour)
9th Lancashire Fusiliers
1st Australian Pioneers
10th Battalion, Australians
11th Battalion, Australians
12th Battalion, Australians
7th Battalion, Australians
91st King's Own Scottish Borderers
6th East Yorkshire Regiment (Pioneers)
313th Road Construction Company, R.E.
2nd/8th West Yorkshire Regiment (The Prince of Wales's Own)
2nd/7th Duke of Wellington's Regiment (West Riding)
16th Rifle Brigade (Prince Consort's Own)
85th Labour Company
102nd Labour Company
2nd/6th Duke of Wellington's Regiment (West Riding)

117th Infantry Brigade (two companies)
2nd/4th York and Lancaster Regiment
2nd/5th York and Lancaster Regiment
2nd/6th West Yorkshire Regiment (The Prince of Wales's Own)
2nd/7th West Yorkshire Regiment (The Prince of Wales's Own)
141st Labour Company
3rd R.W.I.R. (British Royal West Indies Regiment)
12th King's Own Yorkshire Light Infantry (Pioneers)
65th Labour Company
2nd/7th Lancashire Fusiliers
2nd/4th East Lancashire Regiment
161st Labour Company
154th Labour Company
9th Gordon Highlanders (Pioneers)
11th Hampshire Regiment (Pioneers)
1st/4th Prince of Wales Volunteers (South Lancashire) (Pioneers)
65th Labour Company
107th Labour Company
102nd Labour Company
17th Northumberland Fusiliers
16th Royal Irish Fusiliers (Pioneers)
87th Labour Company
192nd Labour Company
134th Queen's Labour Company
197th Labour Company
1st/5th Duke of Cornwall's Light Infantry (Pioneers)
261st Labour Company
141st Labour Company
31st Labour Company
19th Lancashire Fusiliers Pioneers
121st Labour Company
8th King's Own Yorkshire Light Infantry (Inf.)
2nd Argyll and Sutherland Highlanders (Princess Louise's) (Inf.)
20th Royal Fusiliers (City of London Regiment) (Inf.)
10th Duke of Wellington's Regiment (West Riding) (Inf.)
12th/13th Northumberland Fusiliers (Inf.)
1st Lincolnshire Regiment (Inf.)
5th Cameronians (Scottish Rifles)
1st Queen's Own Cameron Highlanders

18th King's Regiment (Liverpool)
1st Sherwood Foresters (Nottinghamshire and Derbyshire Regiment)
5th Provisional Cavalry Pioneer Battalion (from R.C.D., Fort Garry Horse, Lord Strathcona's Horse, 9th Hudson Horse, 8th Bengal Lancers, 17th Lancers, Essex Yeomanry, some Hussars, Dragoon Guards and Life Guards)
19th King's Regiment (Liverpool)
9th Seaforth Highlanders (Ross-Shire Buffs, The Duke of Albany's)
260th Labour Company

1918

59th Labour Company
32nd Labour Company
33rd Labour Company
90th Labour Company
70th Kumaon Indian Labour Company
79th Command Company (Indians)
74th Labour Company
65th Italian Labour Company
83rd Labour Company
64th Italian Labour Company
10th Royal Dublin Fusiliers
Chinese Labour Company
61st Labour Company
13th Royal Irish Fusiliers (Princess Victoria's)
84th Labour Company
1st East Yorkshire Regiment
2nd Royal Scots Fusiliers
18th Corps Reinforcement Camp
2nd Wiltshire Regiment (Duke of Edinburgh's)
70th K.I. Labour Company
1st Entrenching Battalion
11th Durham Light Infantry (Pioneers)
14th Royal Irish Rifles
2nd/8th Royal Warwickshire Regiment (15th Entrenching Battalion)
86th Labour Company
85th Labour Company
King's Regiment (Liverpool)

Durham Light Infantry (Pioneers)
10th Royal Irish Rifles
54th Prisoners of War Company
1st Middlessex Alien Labour Company
4th Middlessex Alien Labour Company
55th Chinese Labour Company
76th Skilled Chinese Labour Company
38th Labour Company
191st Labour Company
1st Canadian Reserve Park (Transport)
85th Chinese Labour Company
101st Chinese Labour Company
13th Battalion Transport
69th Labour Company
65th Labour Company
148th Labour Company
13th Labour Company
138th Labour Company
78th Labour Company
Engineering Battalion, 30th Division, U.S. Army
168th Labour Company
12th Labour Company
14th Labour Company
114th Labour Company
6th Middlessex (Alien) Labour Company
168th Labour Company
83rd Labour Company
90th Labour Company
78th Burmese Labour Company
21st Labour Company
714th Labour Company
35th Labour Company

www.ingramcontent.com/pod-product-compliance
Lightning Source LLC
Chambersburg PA
CBHW070843160426
43192CB00012B/2292